PowerPoint® 2007 Just the Steps™

FOR

DUMMIES®

by Barbara Obermeier and Ted Padova

BICENTENNIAL
1807
WILEY
2007
BICENTENNIAL

Wiley Publishing, Inc.

PowerPoint® 2007 Just the Steps™ For Dummies®

Published by
Wiley Publishing, Inc.
111 River Street
Hoboken, NJ 07030-5774
www.wiley.com

Copyright © 2007 by Wiley Publishing, Inc., Indianapolis, Indiana

Published by Wiley Publishing, Inc., Indianapolis, Indiana

Published simultaneously in Canada

For general information on our other products and services, please contact our Customer Care Department within the U.S. at 800-762-2974, outside the U.S. at 317-572-3993, or fax 317-572-4002.

For technical support, please visit www.wiley.com/techsupport.

Wiley also publishes its books in a variety of electronic formats. Some content that appears in print may not be available in electronic books.

Library of Congress Control Number: 2006393474

ISBN: 978-0-470-00981-9

Manufactured in the United States of America

10 9 8 7 6 5 4 3 2 1

WILEY

About the Authors

Barbara Obermeier is principal of Obermeier Design, a graphic design studio in Ventura, California. She's the author of *Photoshop CS2 All-in-One Desk Reference For Dummies* and has contributed as author or coauthor on numerous computer graphics books. Barb is also a faculty member in the Visual Communication Department at Brooks Institute in Ventura.

Ted Padova is the author of more than 25 computer books. He writes primarily on Adobe Acrobat, Adobe Photoshop, Photoshop Elements, and Adobe Illustrator. He is a nationally and internationally known speaker on Adobe Acrobat and digital imaging.

Dedications

I would like to dedicate this book to Gary, Kylie, and Lucky.

— Barbara Obermeier

For Arnie

— Ted Padova

Authors' Acknowledgments

We would like to thank our project editor, Kelly Ewing, who kept the book on track; Bob Woerner, our excellent Senior Acquisitions Editor at Wiley Publishing; Lee Musick, an accomplished technical editor; and the dedicated production staff at Wiley Publishing.

Publisher's Acknowledgments

We're proud of this book; please send us your comments through our online registration form located at `www.dummies.com/register/`. Some of the people who helped bring this book to market include the following:

Acquisitions, Editorial, and Media Development

Project Editor: Kelly Ewing

Senior Acquisitions Editor: Bob Woerner

Copy Editor: Kelly Ewing

Technical Editor: Lee Musick

Editorial Manager: Jodi Jensen

Editorial Assistant: Amanda Foxworth

Sr. Editorial Assistant: Cherie Case

Cartoons: Rich Tennant (`www.the5thwave.com`)

Composition Services

Project Coordinator: Erin Smith

Layout and Graphics: Brooke Graczyk, Denny Hager, Barbara Moore, Heather Ryan, Ronald Terry, Erin Zeltner

Proofreader: Melissa D. Buddendeck

Indexer: Ty Koontz

Anniversary Logo Design: Richard Pacifico

Publishing and Editorial for Technology Dummies

Richard Swadley, Vice President and Executive Group Publisher

Andy Cummings, Vice President and Publisher

Mary Bednarek, Executive Acquisitions Director

Mary C. Corder, Editorial Director

Publishing for Consumer Dummies

Diane Graves Steele, Vice President and Publisher

Joyce Pepple, Acquisitions Director

Composition Services

Gerry Fahey, Vice President of Production Services

Debbie Stailey, Director of Composition Services

Contents at a Glance

Welcome to Microsoft Office PowerPoint 2007. This industry-leading program has an abundance of tools and commands to satisfy all your presentation needs. Whether you want to present important material to your colleagues or clients or just show off your latest travel photos, *Microsoft Office PowerPoint 2007 Just the Steps For Dummies* has something for you.

About This Book

This book cuts all the fluff out of a computer book and takes you right to steps to produce an effect, task, or job. The book is not linear. However, in some cases, you may need to move around a little to understand one concept before moving to another. Each series of steps is defined with headings to simplify your task of searching for a specific item and finding similar tasks related to a particular concept. Be certain to look back at the Table of Contents when you aren't certain where to find one task or another.

Whenever you want to get something done with this book, try to discipline yourself to follow this method:

1. **Pick the task.** Glance over the Table of Contents to find a category you want to explore — something like working with pictures, which we cover in Chapter 9.

2. **Find it fast.** This step is easy because the chapters are designed with coverage of similar items within each chapter. Look over the subheadings listed in the Table of Contents to find a specific task within a given chapter.

3. **Get it done.** Mimic each step and look at the accompanying figures to help you thoroughly understand a given task.

Why You Need This Book

Microsoft PowerPoint 2007 is one of those programs that many people need and use, but they often know only enough to get by. What happens when you want to implement something you haven't used before, like hyperlinks or sound? Most programs today don't come with written documentation anymore. You'll probably have to search through skimpy online Help files or,

Introduction

Conventions used in this book

➟ We use the ➪ symbol for menu commands. This arrow tells you to follow the path to choose a menu command. Something like "Choose Format➪Background" is our way of saying "Choose the Background command from the Format menu." When you select this particular menu command, the Background dialog box opens.

➟ Web site addresses appear in a monospace font to make them easy to identify — for example — `www.dummies.com`. Type the URL in your Web browser's Location bar exactly as you see the monospace type.

➟ To help clarify steps, some figures contain a circle or callout symbol. Look carefully at each figure to fully understand what we're talking about in the text.

 Look for this icon to find tips, notes, and special points of interest throughout the text.

worse, wade through lots of tedious narrative text in a gigantic reference manual to find the help you need.

This book eliminates background descriptions and detailed explanations and takes you directly to a series of steps to produce precisely what you want to do with a presentation. If you want it simple, fast, and direct, then this book is for you.

How This Book Is Organized

This book is organized into four parts. The following sections introduce each one.

Part 1: Creating a Presentation

If you're fairly new to PowerPoint, the chapters in this part get you up and running. First, you find out how to create a presentation. After your presentation is started, we show you how to add content from scratch, from Word, and from existing presentations. You then find the necessary steps on how to edit and format your content to get just the look you want. We finish this part by giving you information on working with the various types of masters in PowerPoint.

Part 11: Adding Visual Interest to Slides

After you have a basic presentation, you may want to add elements to increase visual interest. These comprehensive chapters show you how to do just that. You find out how to add and edit simple graphics like shapes, lines, and arrows. You then find steps on how to add embellishments, such as shadows, glows, and 3-D effects, to those shapes and also to text. If that isn't enough, you discover how to jazz up your text by using the WordArt feature. We also give you all the steps you need to know on how to apply color, texture, and pattern to your slide elements. Pictures score big with added visual punch. We show you how to bring in both clip art and photos to your

presentations. Finally, we round out this part by giving you all you need to create and fully edit tables, and SmartArt such as charts, organizational charts, and diagrams.

Part 111: Adding a Dash of Pizzazz with Multimedia

If text, shapes, and pictures aren't enough for you, you may want to explore using sound, movies, and animation in your presentations. Using multimedia isn't nearly as complicated as you may think. We give you the steps to insert sound and movie files from various sources. You also find out how to use hyperlinks to jump to other slides and presentations or to a Web site. To make your presentation flow smoothly, we show you how to implement transitions between your slides. And lastly, to make your presentation really come alive, you find steps on animating slides, objects, and text.

Part 1V: Presenting Effectively

When your presentation is ready, we show you how to prepare and share it with the world. You find important information on setting up your show options for optimum performance. We give you the steps on printing your slides, handouts, and notes for your audience. You find out how to package your presentation on CD and how to hold an online presentation meeting. We also give you the lowdown on how to save a presentation in the new XML Paper Specification format. Finally, you discover how to give a presentation live or via a kiosk.

Get Ready To . . .

Glance over the Table of Contents to locate the task you want to perform in Microsoft Office PowerPoint. You don't need to grasp any background information; just jump into the series of steps that defines a solution for a project you want to complete.

Part I
Creating a Presentation

Getting Started with PowerPoint

Chapter 1

*T*he first step of any journey through PowerPoint is to start up the program and either create a new presentation or open an existing presentation. Obviously, you can't do anything in PowerPoint until you launch the program.

In this chapter, we talk about some methods you can use to launch PowerPoint and how you can immediately begin to create a new presentation. We also show you how to save a presentation after you've created it and safely exit the program.

Note that, at this point, we assume that you have installed either the entire Microsoft Office 2007 suite or just Microsoft Office PowerPoint 2007. If you need to perform an installation, refer to the user documentation accompanying your installer CD for installation instructions.

Get ready to . . .

Start PowerPoint Using the Start Menu

1. Start your computer and log on to Windows if your computer is not on.

2. Choose Start⇨All Programs⇨Microsoft Office ⇨ Microsoft PowerPoint 2007 (see Figure 1-1). Microsoft PowerPoint opens, and you're ready to create a new slide presentation or open an existing presentation.

Start PowerPoint Using Keyboard Shortcuts

1. Hold the Ctrl key down and press Esc.

2. Press the P key on your keyboard to select All Programs.

3. Press right, left, up, and down arrows to navigate through the menu commands and folders until you arrive at Microsoft PowerPoint 2007.

4. Press Enter to launch PowerPoint, and the PowerPoint default window appears (see Figure 1-2).

 You can also create a program shortcut on your desktop. Locate Microsoft PowerPoint 2007 on your Start menu and right-click the PowerPoint application icon to open a context menu. Choose Send To⇨Desktop (Create Shortcut). The program shortcut is created on your desktop. Just double-click the shortcut icon and PowerPoint launches.

Figure 1-1: Open the Start Menu and choose Programs⇨Microsoft Office⇨ Microsoft PowerPoint 2007.

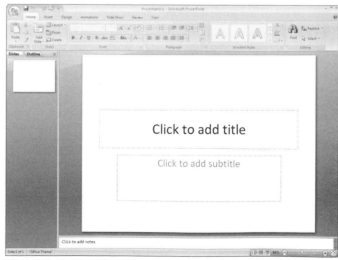

Figure 1-2: The PowerPoint window.

Open a Saved Presentation

1. Launch PowerPoint.

2. Click the Microsoft Office button and choose Open (see Figure 1-3). Alternately, you can press Ctrl+O to open the Open dialog box.

3. Using the Look-in drop-down menu, navigate to your hard drive and locate the folder where you have a saved presentation.

 If you previously worked on PowerPoint files, a list of Recent Documents appears in the Microsoft Office menu to the right of the menu commands. Select a file in the list and it opens in PowerPoint.

4. Choose List from the View drop-down menu to display slide presentations in a list (see Figure 1-4).

5. Click a presentation to select it.

 If you want to open multiple presentations, press the Ctrl key and click each presentation you want to open in the Open dialog box. Click Open, and PowerPoint opens all the selected presentations.

6. Click Open, and the presentation opens in PowerPoint.

Close a Presentation

1. Open a PowerPoint document in PowerPoint.

2. Open the Microsoft Office menu and choose Close. Be certain to not click the X appearing in the top-right corner of the Document window. If you click this X, the program quits.

 Alternately, you can choose File⇨Close to close the document. After closing a file, PowerPoint remains open and ready for you to create a new presentation or open another presentation.

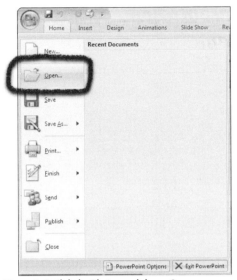

Figure 1-3: Click the File icon and choose Open

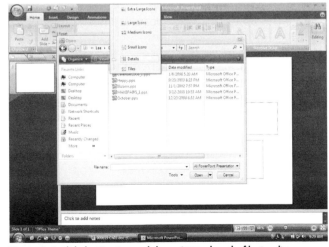

Figure 1-4: Click the View icon and choose List to show the files in a list

Create a Presentation

1. Open PowerPoint.

2. Click File to open the drop-down menu.

3. Click New to open the New Presentation Wizard (see Figure 1-5).

 Alternately, you can press Ctrl+N, and PowerPoint opens a blank new slide. If you want to begin working on a new presentation, start with the document that appears when you press Ctrl+N or double-click the Blank Presentation icon.

4. In the New Presentation task pane (see Figure 1-5), select one of the following options to create a presentation:

   • **Installed Templates:** Click Installed Templates to display all the templates installed with PowerPoint that reside locally on your computer (see Figure 1-6).

   • **Microsoft Office Online**: Click any one of the categories listed below Microsoft Office Online to display templates that you can download from Microsoft. For standard PowerPoint presentations, click the Presentations link and click a subcategory in the middle pane in the New Presentation Wizard.

5. To create a blank presentation, double-click the Blank Presentation icon in the New Presentation Wizard.

Figure 1-5: Click File and click New to open the New Presentation task pane

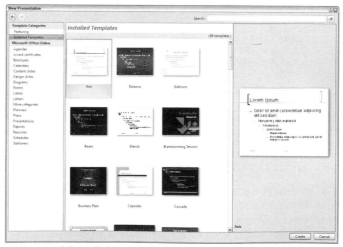

Figure 1-6: Click Installed Templates to browse the templates installed with PowerPoint

Create a Presentation Based on a Template

1. Open PowerPoint.

2. Click File to open the drop-down menu.

3. Click New.

4. Click Presentations under the Microsoft Office Online category (see Figure 1-7).

5. Click Business in the right pane on the New Presentation Wizard.

6. Click a Business template (see Figure 1-8).

7. Click Download.

 The template comes with a rating, tallied from user votes, displayed in the lower right corner. When you click Download, the template downloads from Microsoft's Web site and opens in PowerPoint.

Figure 1-7: Click Presentations in the left pane in the New Presentation Wizard to display a list of presentation categories in the right pane

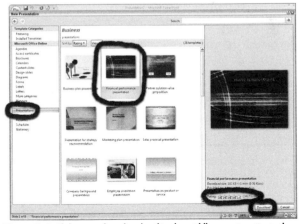

Figure 1-8: Click a template thumbnail in the middle pane to activate the Download button.

Change a Design Template

1. In PowerPoint, open a slide presentation (click File and choose Open).

2. Click the Design tab (see Figure 1-9).

3. Click the More down arrow to open the All Themes window.

4. Move the mouse cursor to a built-in template for your new design (see Figure 1-10).

    PowerPoint provides templates from the following choices:

    - **Search Office Online:** Provides additional templates you can choose from PowerPoint Templates hosted on Microsoft's Web site.

    - **Browse For Themes:** Opens the Choose Theme or Themed Document dialog box, where you can browse your hard drive for themes not shown in the All Themes window.

    - **Save Theme:** Provides an option to save the current selected theme as a new theme to the Document Themes folder. You can use the new Theme in a later design without disturbing the original Theme.

 Clicking a thumbnail changes the current theme to the new theme. You can also examine a theme applied to the current slide by placing the mouse over a thumbnail in the Built-in themes window without clicking the mouse button. As you move the mouse cursor over theme thumbnails, the current slide in view changes background theme designs respective to the mouse position.

Figure 1-9: Click the Design tab to open the All Themes window

Figure 1-10: Click a built-in thumbnail to change the theme

5. Click the template thumbnail for the design you want (see Figure 1-11).

> After clicking a new theme, the slide in view changes the background to the selected theme, and the All Themes window closes. The new theme thumbnail appears in the Design tab.

6. Open a context menu. Right-click the mouse button on the new theme located in the Design tab.

7. Choose Apply To All Slides from the drop-down menu (see Figure 1-12).

> The new current theme is applied to all slides in your presentation having the same slide master. Note that if you have a different master for the opening slide, the changes won't apply to the opening slide master.

PowerPoint offers several menu commands in the context menu. You can choose from

- **Apply To Matching Slides:** Applies the selected theme to all slide masters matching the selected slide.

- **Apply To Selected Slides:** Applies the new theme to just the slides you selected in the Slides pane.

- **Set As Default Theme:** Choose this menu command, and each time you create a blank new presentation, the default theme will be the one you target as the new default.

- **Add Gallery To Quick Access Toolbar:** Adds a drop-down menu in the Quick Access Toolbar, where a pull-down menu displays all the theme thumbnails.

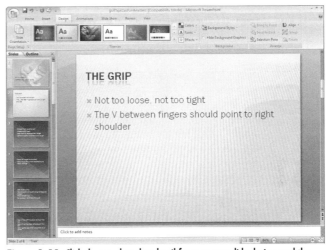

Figure 1-11: Click the template thumbnail for your new slide design, and the selected design is applied to the slide in view

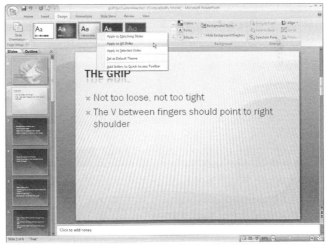

Figure 1-12: Open a context menu (right-click the mouse button) and select Apply To All Slides; the new design is applied to all slides having the same master

Change the Opening Default View

1. Open PowerPoint and click the Design tab.

> When you open PowerPoint, the current default theme is used on a blank new slide. If no slide appears in the PowerPoint window, open the Microsoft Office drop-down menu and choose New. Double-click the Blank Presentation icon to open a slide with the current default theme. (You can't change a theme to a new default without at least one slide appearing in the PowerPoint window.)

2. Open a context menu on the new theme you want to appear as your new default.

> If the theme you want to use doesn't appear in the Design tab, click the More down arrow to open the All Themes window. Select a new theme, and the theme thumbnail moves to the Design tab. At this point, you can open a context menu on the thumbnail.

3. Select Set As Default Theme (see Figure 1-13).

4. Quit PowerPoint. Press Alt+F4 or click the Microsoft Office icon and choose Exit PowerPoint at the bottom of the drop-down menu.

5. Relaunch PowerPoint. A new blank slide appears with your new default theme design.

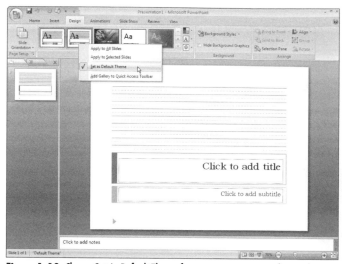

Figure 1-13: Choose Set As Default Theme from a context menu to change the default theme

Save a Presentation

1. Create a new blank presentation or a presentation from a design template.

2. Click Save in the Quick Access Toolbar or open the Microsoft Office menu and choose Save (see Figure 1-14). The Save As dialog box appears.

 Note that you can also click the File icon to open the File drop-down menu and choose Save or press Ctrl+S. PowerPoint opens the Save As dialog box the first time you save a file and prompts you for a filename and a folder location.

3. Name your file by typing a name in the File Name text box and locate a folder where you want to save the file.

4. Click Save to save the file.

Figure 1-14: Click the Save tool or choose Save from the Microsoft Office menu

Change Save Options

1. Open a presentation in PowerPoint.

2. Click File in the Quick Access Toolbar to open a drop-down menu.

3. Click the right-pointing arrow adjacent to the Save As command to open a submenu.

4. Click PowerPoint 97-2003 Format (see Figure 1-15).

5. Type a name, select a folder location, and click Save.

 You can't open PowerPoint 2007 files in earlier versions of PowerPoint. To make the presentations compatible with earlier versions, choose the PowerPoint 97-2003 format.

Exit PowerPoint

1. Click the Close box in an open presentation document.

2. If you haven't saved the file since your last edit, PowerPoint prompts you with a dialog box to save your changes before the file closes (see Figure 1-16).

3. Click Yes to save your last edits. Click No to exit PowerPoint if you want to quit without saving your changes.

 Alternately, you can press Alt+F4 to exit PowerPoint.

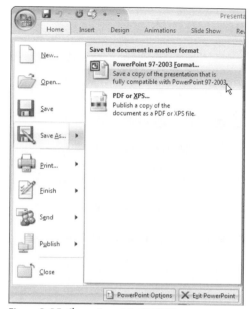

Figure 1-15: Choose PowerPoint 97-2003 to save a presentation that can be opened in earlier versions of PowerPoint

Figure 1-16: Click Yes to save your last edits before exiting PowerPoint or No to ignore edits made since the last save

Customizing the PowerPoint Interface

*P*owerPoint offers you much flexibility in customizing your work environment to suit your own personal editing needs. You can organize toolbars, open frequently used toolbars, and add commands to toolbars. All these options are available so that you can create a work environment that accommodates your slide-creation needs.

In addition to customizing the PowerPoint interface, we tossed in a little information on accessing help documents. After you get a handle on creating a blank presentation — the stuff we discuss in Chapter 1 — things can get a little complicated. Fortunately, PowerPoint offers you help every step along the way as you create your presentations.

Get ready to . . .

Customize Tools

1. Open PowerPoint and click the Microsoft Office icon.

2. Click PowerPoint Options at the bottom of the menu to open the PowerPoint Options window (see Figure 2-1).

3. Click Customization in the left pane and click the down arrow to the right of File under Choose Commands From to open the drop-down menu (see Figure 2-2).

 The menu opens to display a list of the top-level menus by menu name and a list of tools.

4. Click View to display the View menu choices, and the right pane in the PowerPoint Options window changes to reflect the View menu items (see Figure 2-3).

5. Click <Separator> at the top of the menu.

6. Click the Add button in the middle of the Window to add a Separator bar to the right pane.

 Adding a Separator bar divides a new tool group in the Quick Access menu bar from the default tools appearing in the Quick Access Toolbar. You can add as many Separator bars as you like to divide up the tools. Unlike the commands and tools below the <Separator> item, the <Separator> does not disappear from the left pane when you click the Add button. Clicking any item below the <Separator> moves that item to the right pane while removing it from the left pane.

Figure 2-1: Click an item in the left pane and click Add to move it to the right pane

Figure 2-2: Click the down arrow to open a menu where the top-level menu commands and additional tools appear

7. Click a menu item in the left pane. For example, click Normal View in the left pane.

8. Click the Add button to move Normal View to the right pane.

9. Click any other items and click Add after each selection to move several commands to the right pane. In this example, Notes Page View, Slide Master View, and Slide Show are added (see Figure 2-3).

 PowerPoint offers you no provision for selecting multiple items in the left pane to move to the right pane. You must individually select a menu command or tool in the left pane and click the Add button to move the item to the right pane. After moving one item, you then select another and follow the same procedure.

10. Click OK to close the PowerPoint Options window.

11. Click a new tool loaded from the PowerPoint Options window that now appears in the Quick Access Toolbar. The PowerPoint window changes to the new view (see Figure 2-4).

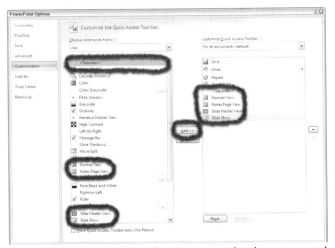

Figure 2-3: Add several commands from the View menu by selecting a command and clicking the Add button

Figure 2-4: Click a new tool loaded in the Quick Access Toolbar to change the view in the PowerPoint window

Reset the Quick Access Toolbar

1. Open PowerPoint.

2. Right-click the Quick Access Toolbar.

3. Choose Customize Quick Access Toolbar from the menu options to open the PowerPoint Options window (see Figure 2-5).

 Notice that you have two ways to open the PowerPoint Options window. Either click the File icon to open the File menu and select PowerPoint Options at the bottom of the menu or open a context menu on the Quick Access Toolbar and select Customize Quick Access Toolbar.

4. Click Reset in the PowerPoint Options window.

 The Quick Access Toolbar returns to the default view when you first launched PowerPoint.

5. Click Yes in the dialog box that prompts you if you're sure you want to restore the Quick Access Toolbar.

6. Click the OK to close the window.

Access Commands with Keyboard Shortcuts

1. Open a slide presentation in PowerPoint.

 You can open any slide presentation you created or use the default presentation that opens when you launch PowerPoint.

2. Press the Alt key on your keyboard to display quick access keyboard shortcuts (see Figure 2-6).

 When you press the Alt key, small boxes with numeric and alpha characters appear aside menus and tools. Press any character respective to a menu or tool to select the menu or tool. If you access a menu, the toolbar changes to reflect options available in that menu, and a new set of numeric/alpha characters appears. Press a character, and the respective action is invoked.

Figure 2-5: Open a context menu on the Quick Access Toolbar and choose Customize Quick Access Toolbar from the menu options to open the PowerPoint Options window

Figure 2-6: Press the Alt key to display the keyboard shortcuts

3. Try using some keyboard shortcuts by first pressing Alt, then press the following characters on your keyboard:

   • Press the W key on your keyboard to open another set of keyboard shortcuts for the View menu options.

   • Press M on your keyboard to display the Slide Master view.

 Practice by clicking the Alt key to access the first level of keyboard shortcuts and press a character on your keyboard to open a menu, access a tool, or change a view.

Add Ribbon Tools to the Quick Access Toolbar

1. Open PowerPoint and click one of the tabs on the Ribbon.

2. Right-click a category bar beneath one of the sections to open the context menu (see Figure 2-7).

3. Click Add to Quick Access Toolbar from the menu options.

4. Click a tab in the Ribbon to display different tools.

5. Right-click to open a context menu on a different tool set name.

6. Click Add to Quick Access Toolbar.

7. Open a menu on a tool added to the Quick Access Toolbar by clicking the icon and making a menu selection (see Figure 2-8).

 Below the Quick Access Toolbar, you find the Ribbon. The Ribbon commands are respective to the tab selected at the top of the Ribbon. For example, click the Home tab, and the Ribbon displays a variety of tools for Clipboard actions, Slides options, text formatting, and editing. Click another tab, and all the tools change in the Ribbon. Below each category of tools, you find a name for the tool set. For example, in the Home tab, you find names across the bottom of the Ribbon for Clipboard, Slides, Font, Paragraph, Word Art Styles, and Editing. Open a context menu on any name of a given tool set, and the context menu includes a command to add the tool set to the Quick Access Toolbar.

Figure 2-7: Open a context menu on a tool set name and select Add To Quick Access Toolbar

Figure 2-8: Click a tool icon to open a menu and make a menu selection

 You can continue adding tools to the Quick Access Toolbar for all frequently used tools. The advantage of adding tools to the Quick Access Toolbar is that you can have one tab displayed with tools in the Ribbon and other tools available in the Quick Access Toolbar. You can select tools from the Quick Access Toolbar without changing the Ribbon view. As tools are added to the Quick Access Toolbar, a down arrow appears adjacent to the tool icon. Click the arrow to open a menu where options for the toolset are selected.

Get Help in PowerPoint

1. Open PowerPoint, and click the Question mark icon on the far right side of the Ribbon or press the F1 key on your keyboard. The PowerPoint Help window opens (see Figure 2-9).

 When accessing help information, you don't need to have a slide document open in PowerPoint.

2. To find help information, do one of the following:

- Type a Help topic to search in the text box adjacent to the Search item in the PowerPoint Help window.

- Click an item in the Table of Contents listed below the Browse PowerPoint Help text in the PowerPoint Help window. When the Topics pane is shown after clicking one of the Table of Contents items, click a topic to review help information respective of the topic.

 If you want a hard copy of a Help item, you can easily print the Help topic window by clicking the Printer icon or pressing Ctrl+P. The Print dialog box opens. Make a selection for your printer and choose the page range for the pages to be printed.

3. Click a Table of Contents item to open a Topics pane listing topic items for the respective Table of Contents item.

4. Click an item in the Topics list, and the Help document displays information on the selected item (see Figure 2-10).

5. To expand the pane so that you can read more comfortably, click the Maximize button in the top right corner of the Help document.

6. To find help on additional topics, click the Home icon in the top left corner of the Help document to return to the Table of Contents pane.

 The Microsoft Office PowerPoint Help document is an independent file. Move the document around by dragging the title bar. Minimize, maximize, and close the Help window by clicking the appropriate button in the top right corner. Note that when you're using online help, help documents are shown from files stored on Microsoft's Web site. If using Help while working offline, documents are displayed from files stored on your hard drive that were added when you installed Microsoft Office 2007.

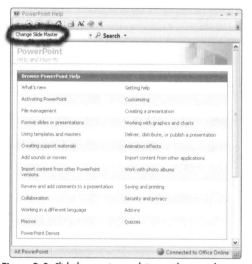

Figure 2-9: Click the question mark icon at the top right corner of the Ribbon or press F1 to open the Help window

Search Help Online

1. Open PowerPoint and click in the question mark icon in the top right corner of the Ribbon or press the F1 key to open the PowerPoint Help window.

2. Type PowerPoint Home Page in the Search text box and press the enter key to open the topics pane with a list of search results.

3. Click PowerPoint Home Page in the topics list.

 When you type PowerPoint Home page in the PowerPoint Help window and press the Enter key, the first item listed in the topics list is PowerPoint Home Page. This text is a link to Microsoft's Web page for PowerPoint information and help. Click the link, and the PowerPoint Home Page on Microsoft's Web site opens in your default Web browser.

 Note that when you open PowerPoint Help, you have many choices from the Search drop-down menu. If you select PowerPoint Help, you change from online help to offline help, and the help documents are accessed from your hard drive. If you select All PowerPoint from the Search drop-down menu, you switch to online help documents.

4. Search for an item on the PowerPoint Home Page by typing keywords in the Search text box in your browser window.

5. Click Search to open a Web page with your search results (see Figure 2-11).

Figure 2-10: Click an item in the topics list to display help information on the respective topic

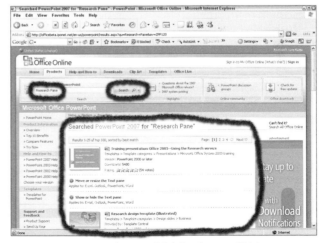

Figure 2-11: Type a search item and click Search in your Web browser to open a Web page listing search results

Use the Research Pane

1. With PowerPoint open, click the Review tab in the Ribbon.

2. Click Research to open the Research Task Pane.

3. Select Translation from the drop-down menu at the top of the Task Pane to open the Translation pane.

4. Type a Word you want to translate at the top of the Research pane.

5. Open the From drop-down menu and select a language you want to translate from.

6. Open the To drop-down menu and select a language you want to translate to (see Figure 2-12).

7. Click the Right arrow adjacent to the search word or press Enter on your keyboard to display the results of the search. Click the X in the upper right corner of the Research Task Pane to close the pane.

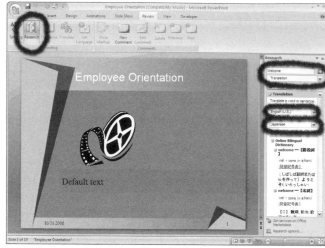

Figure 2-12: Type a word to translate and select a From and To language

 The results of the translation are reported in the Translation pane below the To drop-down menu. Other options you have in the Research pane include a Thesaurus, a Spell Checker, Reference Books, and Research Sites. In the Ribbon, the Thesaurus, Translate, and Set Language items are grayed out. To make these items active, click inside a text item in a slide or in the outline view.

Building Your Presentation and Adding Content

Chapter

3

An outliner, among other things, makes PowerPoint the ideal presentation program. By importing text from a Microsoft Word document or typing text directly in PowerPoint in outline form, you can quickly apply text to slides when preparing a presentation. You can select a design template, type an outline, and finish your presentation within record time. When modifying a presentation is necessary, PowerPoint provides you options for rearranging slides, text on slides, and slide designs without spending time creating new documents.

In this chapter, you find out how to use PowerPoint's outliner feature, assemble quick and easy presentations, and modify your presentation designs.

Get ready to . . .

Create an Outline

1. Launch PowerPoint and create a new blank presentation.

    By default, a blank presentation opens when you launch PowerPoint. If you don't have a new blank slide in view in the PowerPoint Slides pane, click Microsoft Office menu, choose New, and double-click the Blank Presentation icon.

2. Click the Outline tab to show the Outline pane (see Figure 3-1). If the Outline tab is not visible, click the Normal icon in the Ribbon.

3. Click to the right of the small slide icon, type the main title in the title slide, and then do one of the following:

   - **Advance to the next slide:** If you want just a title to appear on the first slide, press Enter, and PowerPoint creates a second slide.

   - **Add a subtitle:** Press Ctrl+Enter, and you stay on the same slide. Type a subtitle and then press Enter. Note that if you want to add a second subtitle to the same slide, just press Enter.

4. Type a slide title on slide 2 in the Outline tab and press Ctrl+Enter to add a bullet point.

5. Press Enter to add additional bullet points.

    After you press Ctrl+Enter to add your first bullet point, you press the Enter key to add additional bullet points on the same slide. When you're ready to move to another slide, press Ctrl+Enter.

6. Press Ctrl+Enter to create a new slide and repeat Step 5 to continue adding slides (see Figure 3-2).

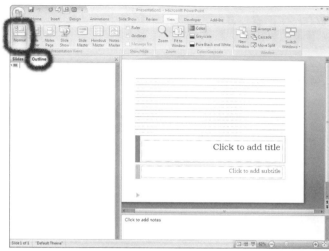

Figure 3-1: Click the Outline tab to open the Outline pane

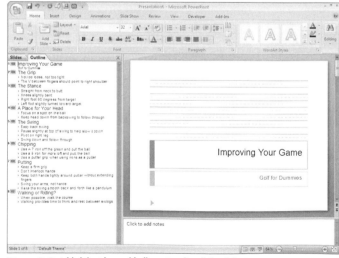

Figure 3-2: Add slide titles and bullet points for all the slides in your presentation

Import a Microsoft Word Document

1. Create a new blank presentation in PowerPoint.

2. Click the Home tab in the Ribbon.

 If you have an outline created in Microsoft Word and formatted as an outline, choose Insert⇨Slides From Outline. PowerPoint imports the Word outline.

3. Click the Add Slide button to open a drop-down menu.

4. Select Slides From Outline in the drop-down menu (see Figure 3-3) to open the Insert Outline dialog box.

5. Navigate your hard drive in the Insert Outline dialog box and select the Microsoft Word file you want to import as an outline.

6. Click Insert in the Insert Outline dialog box.

 Files you import as outlines from Word files should be formatted with styles in MS Word. If you import a file and the level 2 heads don't import as subcategories in PowerPoint, you need to return to the Word file and check the formatting. If you have trouble importing outlines with subheads, save the Word files as Word 2003 documents and try to import again in PowerPoint.

7. Click the Outline tab in PowerPoint to view the outline (see Figure 3-4).

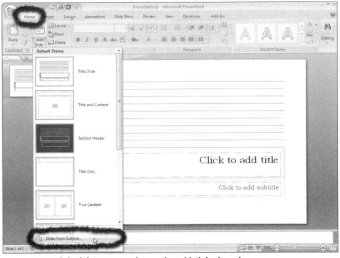

Figure 3-3: Click Slides From Outline in the Add Slide drop-down menu

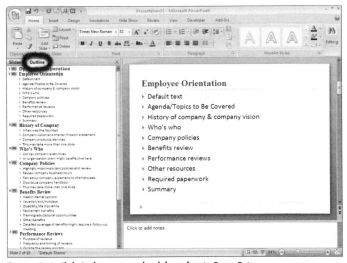

Figure 3-4: Click Outline to view the slide outline in PowerPoint

Send a Presentation from PowerPoint to Word

1. Create a slide presentation in PowerPoint.

2. Click the Microsoft Office button to open the drop-down menu.

3. Select PowerPoint Options to open the PowerPoint Options window.

4. Click Customization in the left pane.

5. Open the Choose Commands From drop-down list and select All Commands.

6. Drag down the scroll bar in the commands list until you see Send To Microsoft Word (see Figure 3-5).

7. Select Send to Microsoft Word and click the Add Button. Click OK to close the window and the Send To Microsoft Word tool is added to the Quick Access Toolbar.

8. Click the Send To Microsoft Word tool in the Quick Access Toolbar (see Figure 3-6).

When you click the Send To Microsoft Office Word tool in the Quick Access Toolbar, the Send To Microsoft Office Word dialog box opens.

Figure 3-5: Open the PowerPoint Options dialog box and select Send To Microsoft Word from the All Commands drop-down menu

Figure 3-6: Click the Send To Microsoft Word tool in the Quick Access Toolbar

9. Click Outline Only in the Send To Microsoft Office Word dialog box (see Figure 3-7). Note that you have other options in the Send to Microsoft Office Word dialog box:

- **Notes Next To Slides:** Export slides and notes to Microsoft Word with the notes appearing adjacent to the right of the slides.

- **Blank Lines Next To Slides:** Export slides with lines next to the slides where you can add your own comments and notes in the Word file.

- **Notes Below Slides:** Export a single slide to a page with notes appearing below each slide.

- **Blank Lines Below Slides:** Places a single slide on each page with lines below each slide.

- **Outline Only:** Exports no slides to Word. The outline text is exported as a Word .doc file.

10. Click OK, and your file is exported directly to Microsoft Office Word. MS Office Word opens automatically, and your outline appears in a new document window (see Figure 3-8).

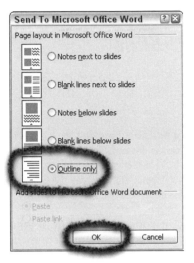

Figure 3-7: Click Outline only

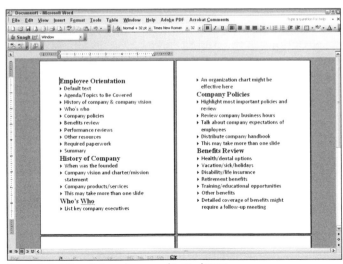

Figure 3-8: A PowerPoint outline opened in Word 2007

Change a Title Slide to a Title and Content Slide

1. Import a Microsoft Office Word document from either an outline or text document into PowerPoint by choosing Add Slide⇨Slides From Outlines.

   When you import a Word file in PowerPoint, the first slide in your presentation assumes the Title layout followed by slides defined as Title and Content. If you have a bulleted list and you want the first slide to appear the same as the remaining slides, you need to change the first slide master to a Title and Content slide.

2. Observe the first slide in your presentation. If you see the text falling off the slide and not appearing within the Title master slide, you need to change the slide master to fit the text (see Figure 3-9). To do so, click the Home tab and click Layout to open a pop-up menu (see Figure 3-10).

3. Select the Title and Content slide master from the options in the pop-up menu.

   Note that you can observe the names of all slide masters in the pop-up menu by moving the cursor over a slide thumbnail. Each slide master has a specific name to identify the master. You find slide masters for Section Header, Title Only, Two Content, Comparison, Blank, Content With Caption, and Picture With Caption in addition to the Title and Title and Content masters.

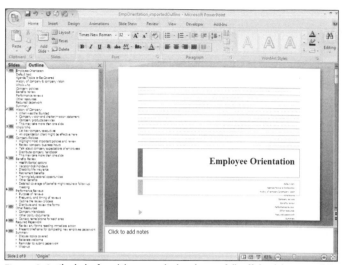

Figure 3-9: Check the first slide to see whether the text falls off the slide or out of the text placeholder

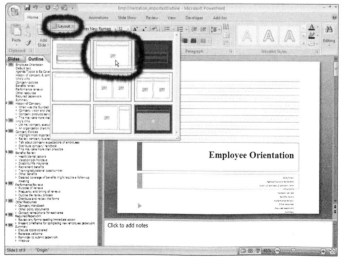

Figure 3-10: Select Title and Content from the Layout pop-up menu

Apply a Built-in Slide Template

1. Create a new presentation or import a Word document in PowerPoint. The slide presentation opens with the default slide template

2. Click the Design tab in the Ribbon.

3. Click the More drop-down menu.

 The More drop-down menu appears at the lower right side of the last slide (to the right) thumbnail in the Design tab. Click the down arrow to open the menu.

4. Click the arrow at the top of the window to open a drop-down menu and choose Built-In from the menu commands.

5. Click the thumbnail image for the design you want in the Built-In thumbnail list (see Figure 3-11).

6. Click the Microsoft Office icon and select Save or click the Save tool in the Quick Access Toolbar to open the Save As dialog box.

7. Type a name for your presentation and locate a folder where you want to save it in the Save As dialog box. Click Save to save your presentation.

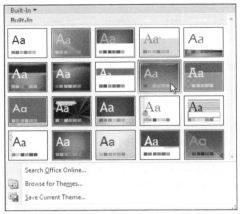

Figure 3-11: Click the design you want to apply to your presentation

Insert a New Slide

1. Open a presentation in PowerPoint.

2. Click the Slides tab to display the slides as thumbnails.

3. Click the slide preceding the slide you want to add in your presentation.

4. Open a context menu by right-clicking the selected slide and then choosing New Slide (see Figure 3-12).

 You can also press Ctrl+M to add a new slide in your presentation or open the Insert tab in the Ribbon and click the Add Slide icon.

5. Type text in either Slide mode or Outline mode for the title and bullet points.

6. Click the Microsoft Office icon and select Save or press Ctrl+S to save your edits.

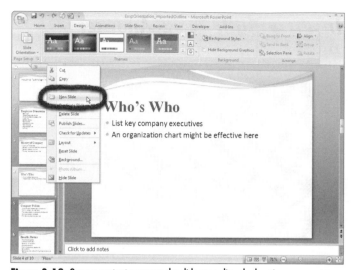

Figure 3-12: Open a context menu on the slide preceding the location you want to insert a new slide and select New Slide

Insert a Slide from Another Presentation

1. Open a presentation in PowerPoint.

2. Click the Slides tab to show the slide thumbnails.

3. Click the Insert tab in the Ribbon to open the drop-down menu.

4. Click Reuse Slides at the bottom of the menu (see Figure 3-13).

    When you click Reuse Slides, the Reuse Slides task pane opens on the right side of the PowerPoint window.

5. Click the Browse button in the Reuse Slides task pane to open the Browse drop down menu. When you open the Browse drop-down menu, you have two menu choices from which to choose:

   - **Browse Slide Library:** Select this menu option and the Select A Slide Library dialog box opens and defaults to the My Slide Libraries folder that is automatically created when you install PowerPoint. As you add slides to your Library, they appear in this folder.

   - **Browse File:** When you select Browse File, the Browse dialog box opens. You can navigate your hard drive in the Browse dialog box and select any PowerPoint Presentation where you want to copy a slide and add it to the current open presentation.

6. Select Browse File from the Browse drop-down menu (see Figure 3-14) to open the Browse dialog box.

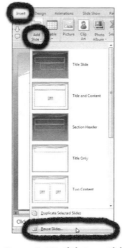

Figure 3-13: Click Reuse Slides at the bottom of the Add slides menu

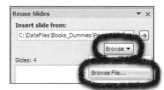

Figure 3-14: Select Browse File from the Browse drop-down menu in the Reuse Slides Task pane

7. Locate a presentation on your hard drive and select it. Click the Open button, and the slides are shown in the Reuse Slides task pane.

8. Move the cursor over a slide you want to add to your open presentation (see Figure 3-15).

     When you move the cursor over a slide, the slide zooms in the Reuse Slides task pane, providing you a better view to carefully examine the slide.

9. Select the slide preceding the location of the new slide you want to add to your presentation in the Slide panel.

10. Click the slide you want to add from the slides shown in the Reuse Slides task pane (see Figure 3-16).

11. Type text on the slide (if so desired).

12. Click the Microsoft Office icon and select Save or press Ctrl+S to save your edits.

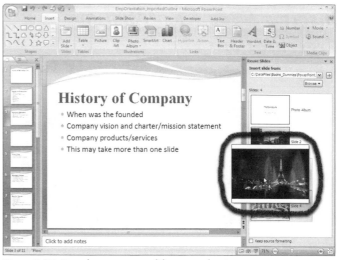

Figure 3-15: Move the cursor over a slide to zoom the view

Figure 3-16: Edit text on the imported slide

Display Multiple Presentations

1. Choose File⇨Open to open a presentation in PowerPoint.

2. Repeat Step 1 until you've opened the files you need.

3. Click the View tab in the Ribbon.

4. Click Switch Windows to open the Switch Windows drop-down menu (see Figure 3-17).

5. Select the presentation you want to view from one of the items listed in the drop-down menu.

Copy a Slide from Another Presentation

1. Open two slide presentations in PowerPoint.

2. Click the View tab and click Arrange All to view both presentations adjacent to each other in the PowerPoint window.

If you want the slides arranged with a particular file appearing on the left side of the PowerPoint window, select the presentation to make it the active window. When you choose Arrange All in the View tab, the active presentation appears on the left side of the PowerPoint window.

3. Click a slide you want to copy in one of the presentations.

4. Open a context menu (right click) on the slide you want to copy and choose Copy from the menu.

5. Click a slide in the target presentation where you want your pasted slide to follow.

6. Open a context menu in the target document and choose Paste. (See Figure 3-18.)

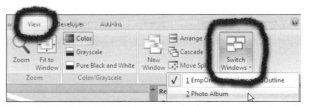

Figure 3-17: Click Switch Windows to open the drop-down menu where all open slide presentations are listed.

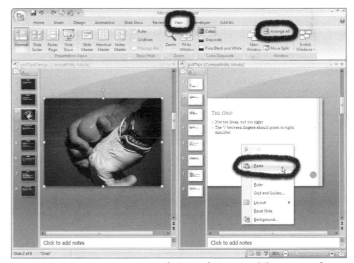

Figure 3-18: Open a context menu in the target document and choose Paste after copying a slide from another presentation.
Photo courtesy PhotoDisc, Inc.

Basic Editing Techniques

*P*owerPoint provides you with a number of editing features you can use to add polish to your presentations. Using a design template starts you off with a particular preset format and layout. When you want to change design and layout, PowerPoint offers you the flexibility to modify text styles, bullet points, tabs and spacing, graphics, and just about any appearance you see on the slides.

In this chapter, you find out how to modify slides by using many PowerPoint commands and tools to customize presentations for your personal taste.

Chapter

4

Get ready to . . .

Edit Text on a Slide

1. Open a presentation in PowerPoint.

2. Click the View tab and click the Normal button.

3. Click the Slides tab to view thumbnail images of the slides in your presentation (see Figure 4-1).

4. Click a slide thumbnail in the Slides tab to display the slide in the Slides pane.

5. Click the cursor inside the text placeholder below the title text placeholder on a slide.

6. Highlight the text you want to edit by dragging the cursor across a line of text.

7. Type new text to replace the selected text.

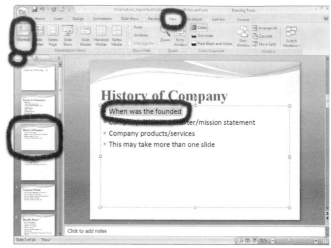

Figure 4-1: Click the Slides tab to view thumbnail images of the slides

Move Text on a Slide

1. With a presentation open in PowerPoint, click a slide in the Slides tab to place a slide in the Slides pane.

2. Click the cursor inside a text placeholder.

3. Move the cursor to the placeholder border so that it changes from an I-beam to a double-crossed arrow and then click the border (see Figure 4-2).

4. Drag the placeholder to a new position.

 Note that when you move a text placeholder, the placeholder moves only on the slide in view. All other text placeholders remain in the positions established on the master slide.

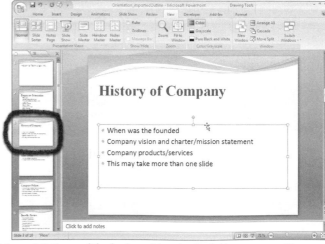

Figure 4-2: You can click a border and drag the placeholder to a new position

Move Text on a Master Slide

1. Open a presentation in PowerPoint.

2. Click the View tab.

3. Click Slide Master.

4. Click a master in the left pane.

5. Click a placeholder and drag it to a new position (see Figure 4-3).

Resize Text Boxes

1. Open a presentation in PowerPoint.

2. Click the View tab.

 If you want to resize a text box on a single slide, select the slide on either the Outline or Slides tab to display the slide in the Slides pane.

3. Click Slide Master.

4. Drag any one of the small circles on the corners or the four squares at the midpoint of each border on the placeholder in or out to size smaller or larger, respectively (see Figure 4-4).

5. Click the View tab and click Normal to return to normal view.

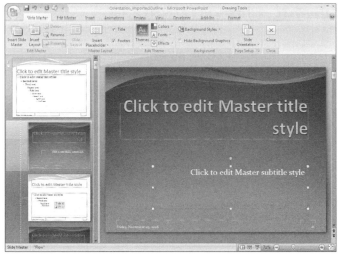

Figure 4-3: Click and drag the placeholder to a new position on the master slide

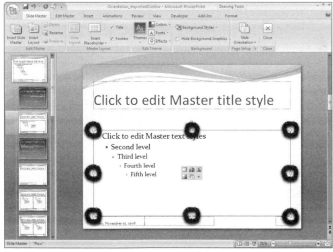

Figure 4-4: Click one of the circles or squares and drag to resize the placeholder

Format Text Attributes

1. Open a presentation in PowerPoint.

2. Click the Home tab if the tab isn't currently in view.

3. Click a slide in the Slides tab where you want to change a text font.

4. In the text placeholder on the slide, right-click the mouse to open a context menu (see Figure 4-5).

5. Choose from the following:

   • **Font:** Open the Font dialog box where various font attributes can be changed.

   • **Font toolbar:** Make font style and font type choices in the Font toolbar appearing above the context menu.

6. Make font attribute choices for selecting a new font and font style.

7. Using the Font toolbar shown in Figure 4-6, do the following:

   • **Change Font:** Click the down arrow to the right of the default font name to open the font menu and select a new font.

   • **Change Point Size:** Click the down arrow to open the point size menu (to the right of the Font menu) and select a new point size.

 Note that you can also type a new point size in the Size text box. You can establish point sizes up to one-half a point size (for example, 52.5).

   • **Change the font style:** Click the B, I or both B and I icons in the Font toolbar to bold and/or italicize the font.

 You can also change font attributes on a master slide in a presentation and apply all changes globally to all slides having the same master. For more information on working with master slides, see Chapter 8.

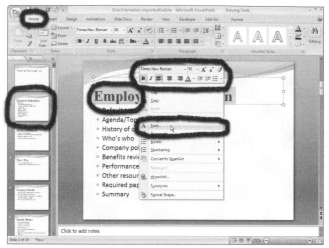

Figure 4-5: Open a slide presentation and select text on a slide

Figure 4-6: Use the Font toolbar to change font attributes

Adjust Line and Paragraph Spacing on a Master Slide

1. Open a presentation in PowerPoint.

2. Click the View tab in the Ribbon.

3. Click Slide Master in the Ribbon.

4. Click the Edit Master tab in the Ribbon.

   Note that the Edit Master tab is only available after you click the View tab and the Slide Master tool in the Ribbon.

5. Select a master slide in the Slides pane.

   All the slide masters are viewable in the Slides pane. Click the master you want to change from those displayed in the Slides tab.

6. Click the cursor in a paragraph you want to edit. Note that you don't need to select all the text in a paragraph, as shown in Figure 4-7.

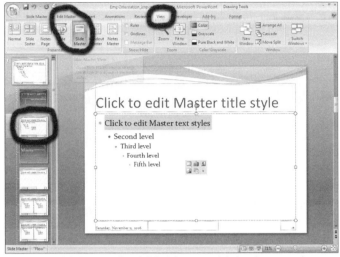

Figure 4-7: Click the View tab and click Slide Master. Click the Edit Master tab to edit a slide master

7. Click the down arrow on the Line Spacing tool to open a menu (see Figure 4-8).

8. Select a preset space option from the menu commands.

 If the amount of line spacing that you want doesn't appear in the menu, click the More option to open the Paragraph menu, where you can apply custom line spacing to the paragraphs on your slides.

9. Click the View tab in the Ribbon.

10. Click Normal in the View tab to view the slide changes.

 If you want to change paragraph spacing on a single slide, be certain not to click the Edit Master tab. While in a slide view, you can select the text within a paragraph and open the Line Spacing menu while viewing the slides with the Home tab open. Any changes made to both text and paragraphs are applied to only the current slide in view.

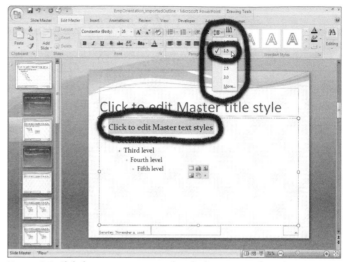

Figure 4-8: Click the cursor in a paragraph and select an option from the Line Spacing drop-down menu to change line spacing

Set Indents and Tabs

1. Open a presentation in PowerPoint.

2. Click the View tab in the Ribbon.

3. Click the Ruler check box in the Ribbon (see Figure 4-9).

4. Drag the sliders in the ruler to reset the tabs.

5. Click the tab selector on the left side of the ruler until the tab you want to use appears. Your choices include the following:

   - **Left tab:** The first marker and default at the top left corner of the slide window, represented by an L shape, is a left tab marker. Left-align text with this tab.

   - **Center tab:** Click the Left tab marker and the tab is changed to a Center tab. Select this tab to center text on the tab marker.

   - **Right tab:** Click the Center tab marker (or click twice when the Left tab marker is shown) and the tab changes to a Right tab marker. Right-align text with this tab.

   - **Decimal tab:** Click the Right tab marker and the tab changes to a Decimal tab. Use this marker to align decimal points.

6. Click inside a paragraph or select multiple paragraphs by dragging the cursor through the text.

7. Click a tab marker on the ruler where you want a tab.

8. Click the Tab Marker Selector to change tabs and click in the ruler where you want another tab. Repeat the steps to add a few different tabs (see Figure 4-10).

Figure 4-9: Click View and check Ruler to show the ruler above a slide

 Click and drag the bottom slider to move the text. Click and drag the top slider to move the bullet. You can also add leading indents by moving the top slider to the right of the bottom slider. To add additional tabs, click the ruler where you want a new tab to appear.

 If you want to change tabs on a single slide, you can click a slide in the Slides pane, click View, and then check the Ruler check box. Adjust the tabs on the ruler, and the new tab settings are applied only to the selected slide. If you want to edit the tabs on a master slide, click the View tab and then click Slide Master. Click Edit Master and select the master slide you want to change in the Slides pane. All new tab adjustments are then applied to the selected slide master.

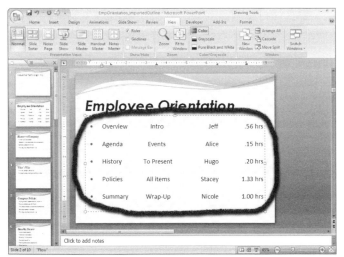

Figure 4-10: Drag tabs in the ruler to move them and click in the ruler to add a new tab

Add a New Text Placeholder

1. Open a presentation in PowerPoint.

2. Click the View tab in the Ribbon.

 Click the Slide Master tab in the Ribbon. Click a slide in the Slides pane where you want to add a new placeholder. Note that default slide masters have a master slide where you find only placeholders for a title and a footer. Use one of these masters when you want to add a placeholder in the body of a slide.

3. Open the Insert Placeholder drop-down menu and select the item you want to insert. If text is what you want, for example, choose Text from the menu commands (see Figure 4-11). Drag the cursor to create a rectangle where the new placeholder will be positioned.

 After you select an item from the drop-down menu, the cursor changes to a crosshair shape. When you see the cursor change, draw a rectangle where you want the placeholder to be located on the slide.

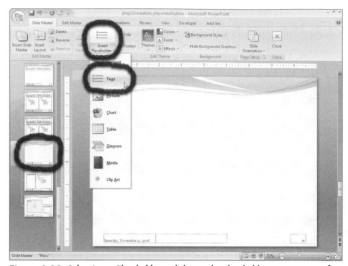

Figure 4-11: Select Insert Placeholder and choose the placeholder type you want from the menu choices

Rotate Text

1. Open a presentation in PowerPoint.

2. Click a slide or slide master containing text you want to rotate in the Slides pane.

3. Click a text placeholder to select it. The rotate handle appears.

 The rotate handle appears at the top of a text placeholder in the middle on the top of the rectangle. When the cursor is positioned above the center handle, the cursor changes to a semicircle with an arrowhead.

4. Position the cursor over the rotate handle, and the cursor changes to a semicircle with an arrowhead.

5. Rotate the text placeholder as you need (see Figure 4-12).

 To constrain movement of the rotation, press the Shift key, and the rotation jumps 15° as you drag the cursor to rotate the box.

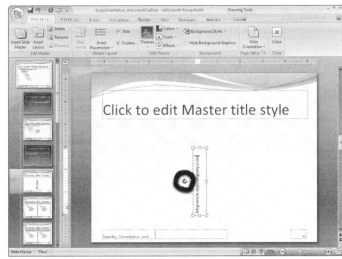

Figure 4-12: Position the cursor over the rotate handle and drag to rotate

View a Slide Show

1. Open a presentation in PowerPoint.

2. Click the View tab and click the Slide Show button or press F5.

    Alternatively, you can click the Slide Show button in the Status bar at the bottom of the PowerPoint window. When you click the Slide Show button in the View tab or press F5, the slide show starts at the beginning of your slide presentation where the first slide in the presentation opens in the slide show view. When you click the Slide Show button in the Status bar, the current slide in view in PowerPoint opens in the slide show view and proceeds to display the show from that slide forward.

3. Click buttons in the lower left corner of the slide show window to do the following:

    Note that the buttons appear in the lower left corner the minute you move the mouse.

   - **Left arrow:** Navigate to the previous slide.

   - **Marker:** Open a pop-up menu where you can mark up a slide with comments or change selection arrow appearances (see Figure 4-13).

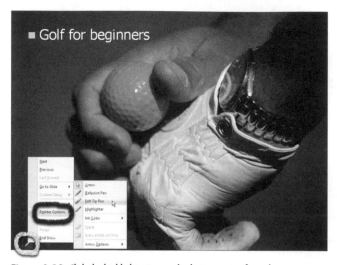

Figure 4-13: Click the highlighter icon and select an option from the pop-up menu
Photo courtesy: PhotoDisc, Inc.

For marking up text with highlights, select the Ballpoint Pen, the Felt Tip Pen, or the Highlighter and drag anywhere on a slide to make a highlight. Use the Eraser tools to eliminate markups. You can change markup colors by clicking Ink Color and selecting a new color from a pop-up color palette.

- **Navigation:** Open a pop-up menu where you can choose navigation and viewing options (see Figure 4-14).
- **Right arrow:** Advance one slide.

4. Press the Esc key to exit Slide Show mode.

If you add markups on slides, PowerPoint opens a dialog box after you press the Esc key to bail out of the Slide Show mode. To keep your markups, click Keep. To remove the markups, click Discard.

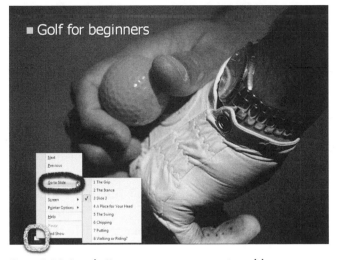

Figure 4-14: Open the Navigation pop-up menu to navigate slides
Photo courtesy: PhotoDisc, Inc.

Organize Slides in the Slide Sorter

1. Open a presentation in PowerPoint.

2. Click View and click the Slide Sorter button.

    Alternatively, you can click the Slide Sorter button in the Status bar. Note that the Slide Sorter button is to the right of the Normal View button and to the left of the Slide View button.

3. Click the Zoom tool in the View tab to open the Zoom dialog box.

4. Click a zoom level radio button or type a value in the Percent text box (see Figure 4-15) and click OK.

5. Click a slide thumbnail and drag it to a location between two slides.

6. When you move a slide either between two slides or to the far left of a slide in a row, a vertical line appears. Release the mouse button, and the slide drops between the slides on either side of the vertical line.

7. Click Normal in the View tab to return to Normal view.

Delete a Slide

1. Open a presentation in PowerPoint.

2. Open the Slides tab.

3. Click a slide thumbnail of a slide you want to delete.

4. Right-click and choose Delete Slide from the context menu (see Figure 4-16).

    Alternatively, you can select a slide in the Slides pane and press the Delete (Del) key on your keyboard to delete a slide.

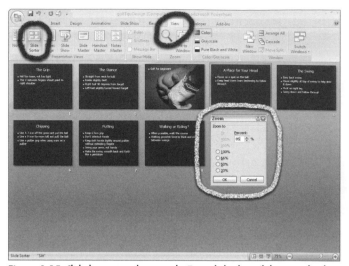

Figure 4-15: Click the zoom tool to open the Zoom dialog box. Click a zoom level, click OK, and then drag a slide to the desired location

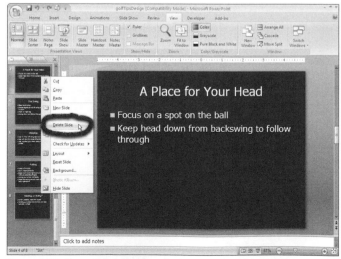

Figure 4-16: Choose Delete Slide from the context menu to delete a slide

Copy and Paste between Slides

1. Open a presentation in PowerPoint.

2. Open the Slides tab and click a slide in your presentation.

3. Right-click to open a context menu on the slide you want to copy.

4. Choose Copy from the menu commands (see Figure 4-17).

5. Open the document where you want to paste a slide.

6. Click the slide preceding the position where you want the new slide to appear to select it.

7. Right-click to open a context menu and choose Paste (see Figure 4-18).

 The pasted slide is inserted in the position immediately after the selected slide. If you inadvertently paste a slide in a different position, open the slide sorter and move the slides around your presentation as desired.

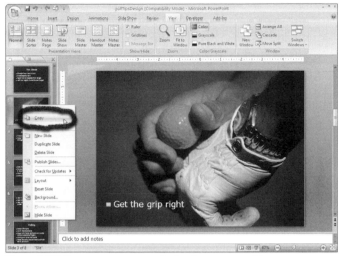

Figure 4-17: Open a context menu and select Copy to copy a slide

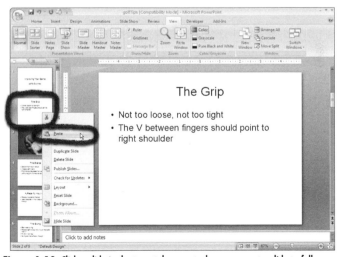

Figure 4-18: Click a slide in the target document where you want a slide to follow and open a context menu and select Paste

Advanced Editing and Formatting

*1*n Chapter 4, we talk about basic editing techniques for changing font attributes on individual slides and master slides. More editing options are available to you for automating your workflow and checking your slides for spelling errors.

In this chapter, we talk about creating headers and footers, automating text formatting and corrections, and using PowerPoint's powerful spell checker.

Chapter
5

Get ready to . . .

Add Headers and Footers

1. Open a presentation in PowerPoint.

2. Open the Slides pane.

3. Click a slide to which you want to apply a header and/or footer.

 Ctrl+click to select multiple slides for adding a header and/or footer if you want headers/footers added to individual slides.

4. Click the Insert tab.

5. Click Header & Footer in the Text area of the Ribbon to open the Header And Footer dialog box (see Figure 5-1).

6. Make choices for the following:

   • **Date And Time**: Check the box, choose a date/time format, and click Update Automatically to make a choice from the drop-down menu.

    If you don't select the Update Automatically radio button, the drop-down menu is inaccessible, and PowerPoint assumes that you want to add your own fixed date format by clicking Fixed and adding a date to the text box below the Fixed radio button.

   • **Update Automatically:** Check the radio button to update the current date each time the presentation is opened.

   • **Fixed:** Click the Fixed radio button and type a date/ time in the text box.

    When you include a date and time in your slide show, the date/time is derived from your system clock. When you add a fixed date/time, you can add any date/time value you desire in the text box, and that date remains fixed no matter when the presentation is opened.

Figure 5-1: The Header And Footer dialog box

- **Slide Number:** Selecting this option automatically adds a slide number to each slide.

- **Footer:** Add a footer by typing the footer text in the box. By default, the footer text appears in the center of a slide.

- **Don't Show On Title Slide:** Check this box to keep the header/footer from appearing on the title slide.

- **Preview:** View the Preview area in the Header and Footer dialog box to see where the header/footer is placed on the slide. Note that when adding a footer as described in this section, three bold rectangles appear at the bottom of the preview thumbnail where the footer information is added.

7. Click Apply, and the header/footer information is applied to the selected slides (see Figure 5-2). Click Apply To All to apply changes to all slides.

 If you need to modify the placement of the header/footer information or the text attributes, click the View tab and click the Slide Master button. Click the Edit Slide Master and scroll the Slides pane to find the master you want to edit. Select the text placeholders and right-click to open a context menu. Select Font to edit the font attributes. From the same context menu, select Paragraph to edit text alignment.

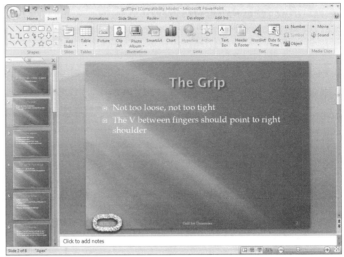

Figure 5-2: Settings made in the Header And Footer dialog box are applied to selected slides

Use AutoCorrections

1. Open a presentation in PowerPoint.

2. Click the Office icon, select PowerPoint Options, and click Customization in the left pane.

3. Open the File menu in the Choose Commands From drop-down menu and select Commands Not In Ribbon.

4. Select AutoCorrect Options from the list, click the Add button (see Figure 5-3), and click OK.

5. Click the AutoCorrect tool in the Quick Access Toolbar to open the AutoCorrect: <Language> dialog box.

 <Language> represents the current language installed as your default language.

6. Choose options from the AutoCorrect tab in the AutoCorrect: <Language> dialog box for those items you want active as auto correction features (see Figure 5-4).

7. Click the AutoFormat As You Type tab and make choices for the kind of auto-formatting you want to use when creating presentations.

8. Click Smart Tags to open the Smart Tags tab.

9. Check the Smart tags you want added to a presentation.

 Click the More SmartTags button to open a Web page on Microsoft's Web site to learn more about smart tags and how to use them in your presentations.

10. Click OK in the AutoCorrect: <Language> dialog box to accept all changes made in the three tabs.

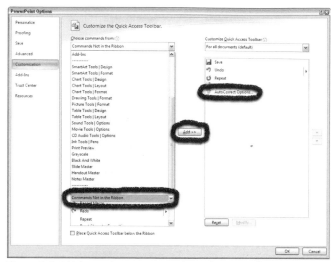

Figure 5-3: Add the AutoCorrect Options to the Quick Access Toolbar

Figure 5-4: Check the options you want to use in the three tabs contained in the AutoCorrect: <Language> dialog box

Use AutoCorrect

1. Open a presentation in PowerPoint.

2. Click the AutoCorrect Options tool in the Quick Access Toolbar.

 Be certain you load the toolbar in the Customize PowerPoint Options dialog box.

3. Click the AutoCorrect tab to open the AutoCorrect: <Language> dialog box.

4. Select options by checking the boxes for the items you want PowerPoint to autocorrect as you type.

5. Type an item in the Replace text box and a replacement item in the With text box. For example, type *Dummy* in the Replace text box and *Dummie* in the With text box. Each time you type Dummy, the word Dummie is automatically substituted. (See Figure 5-5.)

 Adding custom options are in addtion to the autocorrection Power-Point provides automatically as words are checked against the PowerPoint dictionaries.

6. Click the Add button for each item you add for replacement.

7. Click Exceptions to open the AutoCorrect Exceptions dialog box (see Figure 5-6).

8. Click the INitial CAps tab.

9. Type words you don't want PowerPoint to correct when typed, such as a word like E-Mail.

10. Click OK in the AutoCorrect Exceptions dialog box.

11. Click OK in the AutoCorrect: <Language> dialog box.

Figure 5-5: Select items you want PowerPoint to autocorrect

Figure 5-6: Click Exceptions to open the AutoCorrect Exceptions dialog box

 Choices you make in the AutoCorrect: <Language> dialog box and the AutoCorrect Exceptions dialog box become new defaults and apply to all presentations you create and/or edit.

Spell Check Slides

1. Open a presentation in PowerPoint.

2. Click Review in the Ribbon (see Figure 5-7).

3. Click Spelling to open the Spelling dialog box (see Figure 5-8).

4. Click one of the following:

   • **Ignore/Ignore All:** Click Ignore to ignore a word you know is spelled correctly. Click Ignore All if the word is repeated in your presentation.

   • **Change/Change All:** Accept PowerPoint's suggestion in the Change To text box by clicking Change or Change All. If PowerPoint provides no suggestion, type the correct spelling in the Change To text box.

   • **Add:** Click Add if you want to add a word to a custom dictionary.

   • **Suggest:** Click Suggest, and PowerPoint provides one or more options in the Suggestions list.

   • **AutoCorrect:** Click AutoCorrect to add a word to the AutoCorrect list. When you type the word again on a slide, PowerPoint autocorrects any misspelling you might type for the word.

   • **Close:** Click Close when finished spell-checking.

   • **Options:** Click Options to open the PowerPoint Options dialog box where you can edit AutoCorrections Options and add words to a custom dictionary.

5. Click Close after performing a spell check.

Figure 5-7: Click Review and click Spelling to open the Spelling dialog box.

Figure 5-8: Make choices for correcting words to either accept or ignore words not found in the PowerPoint dictionary

The PowerPoint Options dialog box enables you to create multiple custom dictionaries where you can add words that may not be available in the default PowerPoint dictionary. You can add proper nouns, scientific names, special words related to your industry, and more to a custom dictionary.

Find and Replace Words

1. Open a presentation in PowerPoint.

2. Click the Home tab in the Ribbon.

3. Click Editing on the far right side of the Ribbon to open a drop-down menu (see Figure 5-9).

4. Click Replace to open the Replace dialog box.

 When you click Editing and open the drop-down menu, you have choices for Find and Replace. If you want to find a word in a presentation, you can use the Find dialog box. However, using the Replace dialog box offers you the options for finding words as well as replacing words. As a matter of default, use the Replace dialog box when searching for words, and you can always choose to replace a word or just find it.

5. Type a word you want to find and/or replace in your presentation in the Find What text box (see Figure 5-10).

6. Check the following boxes to narrow your search:

   • **Match Case:** Check this box to match letter case.

   • **Find Whole Words Only:** Check this box to locate whole words and not word stems.

7. Click Find Next to find the next occurrence of the word.

8. If you choose to replace a word, type the word that you want as the replacement word and do one of the following:

   • Click Replace to replace a single instance of the found word. You can click the Find Next button to locate another instance.

   • Click Replace All to replace all instances of a found word.

9. Click Close after finding and/or replacing all your searched words.

Figure 5-9: Type a word to find in the Find What text box

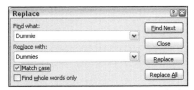

Figure 5-10: Click Close when finished finding and/or replacing words

Copy Text Formatting Using Format Painter

1. Open a presentation in PowerPoint.

    If you want to copy formatting from one presentation to another, open a second presentation.

2. Click the Home tab in the Ribbon.

3. Click the cursor in a text placeholder whose formatting you want to copy and apply to a different slide or different presentation.

4. Open a context menu (right-click) and click the Format Painter tool (see Figure 5-11).

    Alternately, you can also click the Format Painter tool in the Ribbon in the Clipboard area on the far left of the Ribbon.

5. Click a slide in the Slides pane to which you want to apply the same style or a slide on another presentation.

6. When you click the Format Painter tool, the cursor changes to an I-beam with a paintbrush. Move the cursor to a text placeholder and drag across the text line to which you want to apply the copied style. The same text attributes (font style, point size, color, and bullets) from the text you originally clicked with the Format Painter tool are applied to the target slide (see Figure 5-12).

    If you want to apply a style to several slides, double-click the Format Painter tool. Click and drag across text you want to change. Press the Page Down key to scroll slide pages and select more text to change. Repeat the steps to change all the text you want to change. When you finish, click the Format Painter tool again to turn it off or press the Esc key.

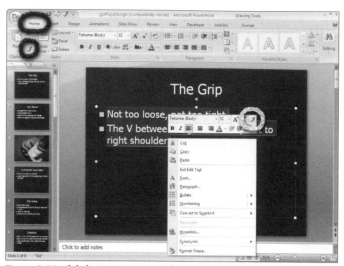

Figure 5-11: Click the Format Painter tool

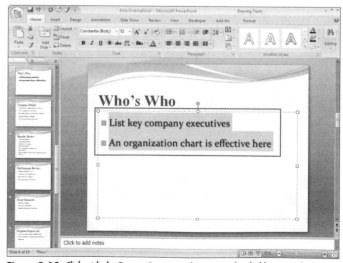

Figure 5-12: Click with the Format Painter tool in a text placeholder to apply the copied style to another slide

Working with Masters

Master slides give you options for globally changing the design of your presentations. With a quick reorganization and formatting for text — or a change in the graphic images on a master slide — you can apply changes to all slides in your presentation in a matter of minutes.

PowerPoint provides you with many different master slides that you can duplicate, revise, and create new masters. The slide master affects the design of your presentation. The note master and handout master handle the designs for notes and handouts.

In this chapter, you find out how to edit and change all master slides and apply the changes to your presentation.

Chapter

6

Get ready to . . .

Create a Master Slide

1. Create a new blank slide presentation by opening the Office menu and choosing New.

2. Double-click Blank Presentation in the New Presentation dialog box to create a presentation with the default master slides.

3. Click View in the Ribbon.

4. Click the Slide Master button in the Ribbon.

5. Click Insert Slide Master (see Figure 6-1).

6. Delete all items on the new slide master you don't want to use by clicking a placeholder and pressing the Delete key. We deleted all items but the footer placeholders on our slide master.

7. Add placeholders by clicking the Insert Placeholder tool drop-down menu and choosing a placeholder from the drop-down menu that appears (see Figure 6-2).

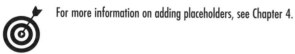 For more information on adding placeholders, see Chapter 4.

8. Click the View tab in the Ribbon and click Normal to return to the slide view.

Figure 6-1: Click Insert Slide Master to create a new master slide

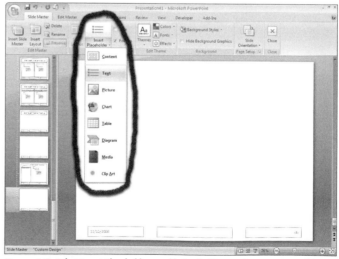

Figure 6-2: Select Insert Placeholder to add placeholders on the new master slide

Apply a Theme to a New Slide Master

1. Create a new master slide in a blank presentation or any presentation you have where you want a new master slide added to the document.

2. Add placeholders for the content you want to display on your new master (see Figure 6-3).

     When you create a new slide master, the new master is added in the Slides pane below all the other masters for a given presentation. You can add additional masters that will be nested in the same group as your new slide master. You can also add multiple variations of slide masters to a presentation.

3. Select the new slide master in the Slides pane.

4. Click Themes in the Ribbon to open the Themes drop-down menu.

     Note that you need the Ribbon view to appear with the Slide Master tab selected in order to use the Themes options.

5. Select a Theme from the Built-In Themes options (see Figure 6-4).

     When you select a Theme and apply the new theme to a new master slide, all masters within a given theme are added to your new master. The master slides appearing in a hierarchy with all masters within a theme are displayed as child items below the parent new master, as shown in Figure 6-4.

6. Click View and click Normal to return to Normal view.

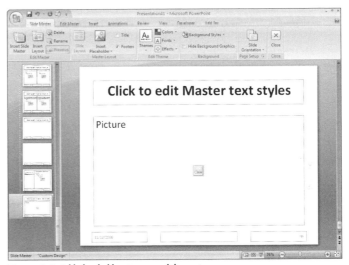

Figure 6-3: Add placeholders to a new slide master

Figure 6-4: Select a Theme to apply to a new master slide

Apply a Slide Master to a Slide

1. Open an existing presentation or create a new presentation in PowerPoint.

2. Add a new slide master to your presentation.

3. Add the placeholders you want to use to the new slide master.

4. Apply a new theme to the new slide master.

5. Click View and click Normal to return to Normal view.

6. Click the Home tab in the Ribbon and click the Slides tab in the Slides pane to display the slides.

7. Right-click to open the context menu on the slide you want to apply a new master and select Layout (see Figure 6-5).

8. From the Layout submenu, drag the scroll bar until the new masters are in view in the Layout submenu.

9. Click a slide master you want to apply to the selected slide.

10. Edit the text on the slide while in Slide view.

11. Apply other options (picture, chart, and so on) according to the slide master content. In our example, we added a picture to a slide formatted with a Picture placeholder (see Figure 6-6).

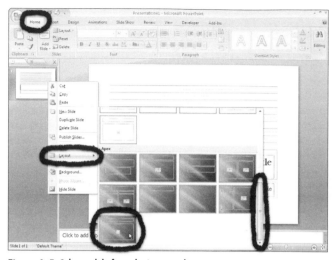

Figure 6-5: Select a slide from the Layout submenu

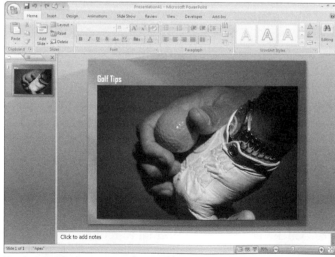

Figure 6-6: Edit the content on the new slide
Photo courtesy PhotoDisc, Inc.

Rename a Master Slide

1. Create a new master slide in an existing presentation or a new blank presentation.

2. While in Slide Master view, click the new slide master to select it.

3. Right-click to open a context menu and choose Rename Master to open the Rename Master dialog box.

4. Type a new name for your master slide in the Rename Master dialog box (see Figure 6-7).

5. Click Rename to rename the master and close the Rename Master dialog box.

Change a Background on a Slide Master

1. Create a new master in an existing presentation or a new blank presentation.

2. Right-click to open a context menu on the new slide master in the Slides pane.

3. Select Background to open the Format Background dialog box (see Figure 6-8).

4. Click a Fill option button for the type of fill you want for the slide background.

5. Select a color from the Preset Colors pop-up menu.

6. Click Apply To All to apply the new background color to all slides using the same slide master.

The Format Background dialog box has many more options for changing backgrounds and setting attributes. You can choose gradient colors, set the amount of stops in a gradient, add transparency, add a shade from the title, and more. For a description of more options choices, see Chapter 8.

Figure 6-7: The Rename Master dialog box

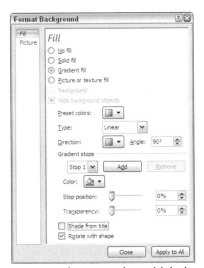

Figure 6-8: The Format Background dialog box

Edit a Notes Master

1. Open an existing presentation in PowerPoint.

2. Click the View tab in the Ribbon.

3. Click the Notes Master button in the Ribbon.

4. Click Background Styles to open the Background Styles pop-up menu (see Figure 6-9).

5. Click a gradient or solid color style you want to appear on the Notes Master.

6. Click Colors to open the Colors pop-up menu (see Figure 6-10).

7. Select a color you want to apply to the Background Style from the color choices in the pop-up menu.

 The Notes Master Ribbon has a number of other options available. By default, all placeholder items are enabled. Remove a check mark to eliminate a corresponding placeholder in the Notes Master Ribbon. Use the Fonts and Effects pop-up menus to change fonts and effects.

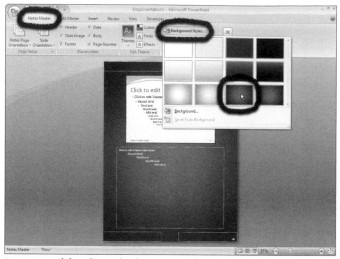

Figure 6-9: Click Background Styles to open the background Styles pop-up menu

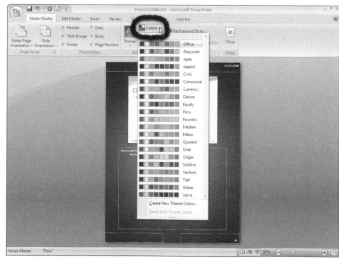

Figure 6-10: Click Colors to open the Colors pop-up menu

Edit a Handout Master

1. Open an existing presentation in PowerPoint.

2. Click View in the Ribbon.

3. Click handout master in the View Ribbon.

4. Click Slide Orientation to open the Slide Orientation drop-down menu.

5. Click Landscape to create a Landscape page (see Figure 6-11).

6. Click Slides-per-page to open the Slides-per-page drop-down menu.

7. Select an option from the menu choices for the number of slides you want to appear on a single page handout (see Figure 6-12).

 If you want a background style and background color, click the Background Styles and Colors buttons to open pop-up menus where you add and change these items.

Figure 6-11: Click Slide Orientation to change the orientation of the handouts

Figure 6-12: Click Slides-per-page to open a menu where the number of slides on a single handout is selected

Part II
Adding Visual Interest to Slides

The 5th Wave   By Rich Tennant

"Look-what if we just increase the size of the charts?"

Adding Lines and Shapes

Chapter

7

*I*f a picture is what you want to use to communicate a message, then PowerPoint's drawing options are your ticket to creating graphic representations of ideas and concepts. Using drawing tools and AutoShapes, you can create visual messages utilizing free-form drawing tools and predefined shapes.

With the ease of drawing lines and geometric shapes or selecting graphic objects from a number of different pop-up menus, you can quickly assemble a diagram or drawing to illustrate your point. In this chapter, you find out how to use the many different tools in PowerPoint to create graphic objects and images.

Get ready to . . .

Use the Drawing Toolbar

1. Create a new blank presentation in PowerPoint by pressing Ctrl+N.

2. Click the text placeholders and press the Delete (Del) key on your keyboard.

3. Click the Insert tab in the Ribbon.

 PowerPoint 2007 moves the drawing tools from a toolbar to a pop-up menu at the left side of the Insert tab.

4. Click the More down arrow to open the drawing shapes pop-up menu (see Figure 7-1).

5. Choose an object from one of the groups.

6. Move the cursor to a slide and drag to create the shape (see Figure 7-2). In this example, the Sun object was selected from the Basic Shapes tool group and drawn on the slide. The tool groups include

   - **Recently used shapes:** Choose from drawing tools used recently in a PowerPoint presentation.

   - **Lines:** Click a Line tool and drag the cursor in the Slide window to create a line. Straight lines, lines with arrowheads, curved lines, polygon lines, and irregular shapes are available in this group.

Figure 7-1: The Drawing tools pop-up menu

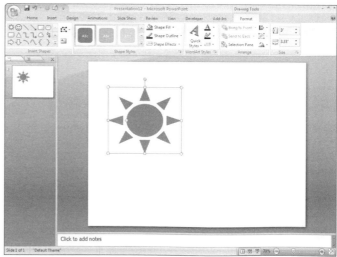

Figure 7-2: Click an object and draw on a slide

- **Rectangles:** Choose from one of the geometric rectangular shapes to create rectangles.

- **Basic shapes:** Ovals, a number of different polygons, special design shapes, and irregular objects are all included in this tool group.

- **Block arrows:** Block arrows offer you choices for various arrowhead shapes for adding emphasis to an item, creating callouts, and working with flowcharts and diagrams.

- **Equation shapes:** Select one of the Equation shapes when you need an object you want to use for mathematical expressions.

- **Flowchart:** Flowcharts are easily created in PowerPoint using the Flowchart objects.

- **Stars and banners:** Choose from a variety of different star shapes or create banners on slides (see Figure 7-3).

- **Callouts:** Choose from many different callout boxes that enable you to associate text with graphic objects (see Figure 7-4).

- **Action buttons:** Action buttons are used to invoke actions such as hyperlinking to other slides, presentations, and Web URLs, playing movies and sounds, and doing other types of link activity.

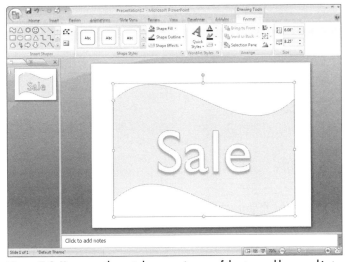

Figure 7-3: You can easily create banners using one of the stars and banners objects

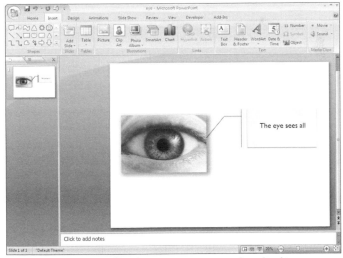

Figure 7-4: You can use callout shapes to associate text and graphic objects

Format a Drawing Object

1. Create a new blank presentation.

    Note that you can also use an existing presentation to follow these steps.

2. Click the Insert tab.

3. Click the More button to open the Drawing pop-up menu and select an object. In this example, we use a callout object.

4. Drag the cursor on a slide to create the drawing shape. In this example, we add a callout to a slide that contains a clip art object.

    For more information on adding clip art to your slides, see Chapter 9.

5. Right-click the drawing object to open a context menu and choose Format Shape to open the Format Shape dialog box.

6. Click Solid Fill in the Format Shape dialog box (see Figure 7-5).

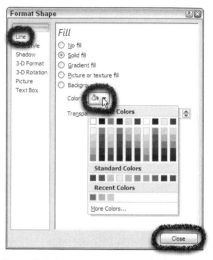

Figure 7-5: Open a context menu and select Format Shape

7. Open the Color pop-up menu by clicking the Color drop-down arrow and select a color.

 The format Shape dialog box provides a number of different options for changing lines and fills. Click items in the left pane and make choices in the right pane for the shape format you want to use.

8. Click Line in the left pane and select a line color in the right pane.

9. Click Close after changing the shape attributes.

10. Select the object and start typing the text you want to appear within the object (see Figure 7-6).

 PowerPoint permits you to start typing when an object is selected without selecting a text tool. After typing text, you can change the font format and style. For more on formatting text, see Chapter 5.

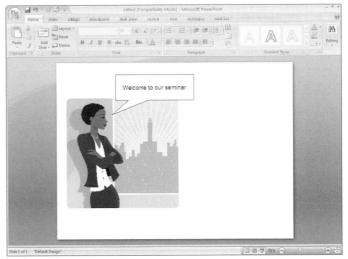

Figure 7-6: Start typing when an object is selected to add text to the object

Use WordArt to Jazz Up Text

1. Create a new blank slide or use an existing presentation.

2. Click the Insert tab in the Ribbon.

3. Click the WordArt button to open the WordArt Gallery (see Figure 7-7).

4. Click a style you want to use for new text on your slide. A WordArt placeholder is automatically added to your slide.

5. Start typing to replace the default text (see Figure 7-8).

6. To edit the WordArt text attributes, choose one of the following:

   • Choose from drop-down menus in the Word Art Styles format area on the Ribbon to change font colors.

   • Right-click the WordArt object to open a context menu and choose Format Shape to open the Format Shape dialog box (refer to Figure 7-5). In the Format Shape dialog box, you can make choices for line, fill, shadow, and 3D appearances.

   • Click the Format tab that appears when you have a WordArt object selected (see Figure 7-8). The Ribbon changes to reflect a number of different tools you can use to change WordArt font attributes.

Figure 7-7: Click WordArt in the Insert tab

Figure 7-8: Type the text you want to appear in the WordArt object

Draw Lines

1. Create a new blank slide.

2. Click the Insert tab on the Ribbon.

3. Click the Shapes drop-down arrow to select shapes.

4. Select a line style from the Lines group (see Figure 7-9). In this example, we use the Elbow Connector line style.

 Note that if you want to create lines at right angles or polygon shapes, you need only find the style to create your shape. In PowerPoint 2007, you'll rarely find a need to draw two lines and group them together to create a single shape.

5. Click the cursor on the slide and drag the mouse with the mouse button depressed to create a line.

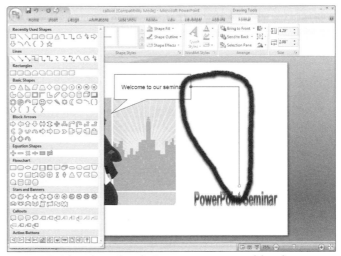

Figure 7-9: Select a line style in the Drawing pop-up menu and drag the cursor on a slide to create the shape

Change a Line Style

1. Create one or more lines on a slide.

2. If creating more than one line, you can select multiple lines and change the format for all selected objects. To select more than one line or object on a slide, click an object and then press Shift + Click. Alternately, for noncontiguous selections, you can use Ctrl + Click for selecting additional objects.

3. Be certain the line (or multiple lines) is selected and then right-click and choose Format Shape from the context menu. The Format Shape dialog box opens (refer to Figure 7-5).

4. Click Line Style in the left pane and select a line style, such as a dashed line (see Figure 7-10).

5. Click Close to exit the Format Shape dialog box.

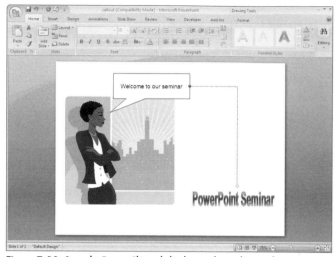

Figure 7-10: Open the Format Shape dialog box to change line attributes

Add Arrowheads to Lines

1. Click the Insert tab in the Ribbon.

2. Click the Shapes down arrow to open the pop-up menu.

3. Select a line shape.

 Note that you have lines available with and without arrowheads. You can choose any open line and apply arrowheads later when formatting the shape. Any line choice you make in the Drawing tools pop-up menu is acceptable when adding arrowheads.

4. Draw a line on your slide.

5. Right-click the line and choose Format Shape to open the Format Shape dialog box (see Figure 7-11).

6. Select Line Style in the left pane and make choices for

   • **Width:** Select a line width from the menu or type a value in the text box.

   • **Arrow Settings:** Open the pop-up menus and make choices for the Begin/End Types and Begin/End Sizes.

7. Click Close to accept the changes.

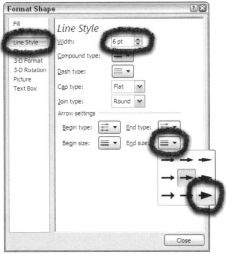

Figure 7-11: Format arrowheads in the Arrows section of the Format Shape dialog box

Create Block Arrows

1. Open a presentation in PowerPoint and select a slide in the Slides tab.

2. Click the Insert tab in the Ribbon.

3. Click the Shapes down arrow to access the drop-down menu of different shapes available.

4. Click a style from within the Block Arrow section and draw the shape on the slide.

5. Right-click the shape to open a context menu and choose Format Shape.

6. Add a gradient fill in the Format Shape dialog box (see Figure 7-12).

 Note that the options available in the Format Shape dialog box are the same as when changing line and other object attributes.

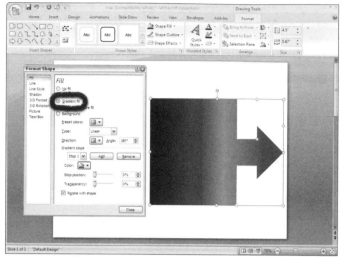

Figure 7-12: Add a gradient fill color to a block arrow

 If you want to add flair to the design of block arrows, click the 3-D Format item in the left pane and select a 3-D format. Additionally, you can add a drop shadow by clicking Shadow and adjusting shadow attributes in the right pane.

Change a Shape

1. Click Insert on the Ribbon.

2. Open the More Shapes menu by clicking the down arrow.

3. Select any drawing shape in the pop-up menu. In this example, we use the Arc tool.

     If you want to create a semicircle, use the Arc tool to create the initial shape. When you release the mouse button, handles appear on the shape. Drag a handle on the top or bottom to a new location to expand an arc to a semicircle.

4. Click and drag the mouse to create the arc shape (see Figure 7-13).

5. After creating the shape, click the line to select it if it's not currently selected.

6. Click the Format tab below the Drawing Tools tab in the Ribbon.

7. Click the Edit Shape tool to open a drop-down menu.

8. Click Change Shape to open a submenu.

9. Click a shape you want to appear as a new shape. In this example, we convert the semicircle to a smiley face (see Figure 7-14).

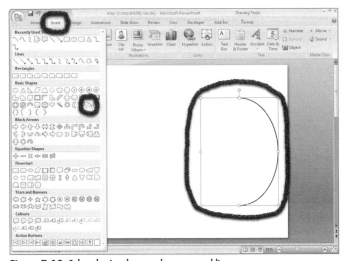

Figure 7-13: Select the Arc shape to draw a curved line

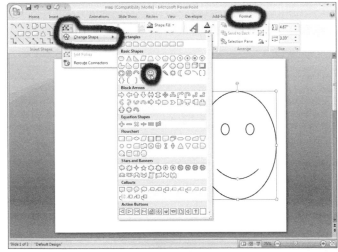

Figure 7-14: Click a new shape in the Change Shape submenu to convert to a new shape

Move Lines and Shapes

1. Create a line or shape on a slide.

2. Move the cursor over a point on the line or shape.

3. Wait until the cursor changes to a selection arrow with a four-headed arrow (see Figure 7-15) and then click and drag to move the line or shape.

4. To nudge a line or shape horizontally or vertically, do one of the following:

   • Select the line or shape and press an arrow key to move in the direction of the arrow key.

   • Select a line or shape and press the Ctrl key and an arrow key to slightly nudge in the direction of the arrow key. The Ctrl key moves a line or object in smaller increments than when you press just the arrow key.

Figure 7-15: Position the cursor over a line and click and drag to move the line

Rotate Lines and Shapes

1. Create a line or shape on a slide.

2. Select the object to reveal its rotate handle and then move the cursor over that handle.

3. Wait until the cursor changes from a selection arrow to a semicircle and arrowhead (see Figure 7-16) and then click and drag to rotate the line or shape.

   Drag left to rotate counterclockwise or right to rotate clockwise.

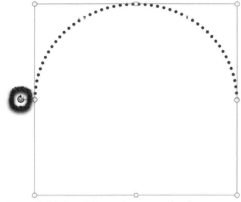

Figure 7-16: Drag left or right to rotate the object

Stack Lines and Shapes

1. Create a blank new slide.

2. Click the Insert tab in the Ribbon.

3. Open the Shapes pop-up menu and click the Line tool.

4. Draw a series of lines to create a map with lines intersecting.

     You can change line defaults by creating a line and setting all line attributes in the Format Shape dialog box. When you have the line formatted, right-click the line to open a context menu and choose Set As Default Line.

5. Press Ctrl+A to select all the lines.

6. Right-click and choose Format Shape to open the Format Shape dialog box.

7. Click Line Style in the left pane and choose 12 from the Width drop-down menu for a 12-point line. Click OK to change all lines to 12 points (see Figure 7-17).

8. Press Ctrl+A to select all the lines. Right-click a selected line, choose Group from the context menu, and then choose Group from the flyout menu to treat all the lines as one unit.

9. While the lines are selected, right-click and open the context menu to choose Copy.

10. Press Ctrl+V to paste a copy of the selected lines.

11. Right-click and choose Format Shape. The Format AutoShape dialog box opens.

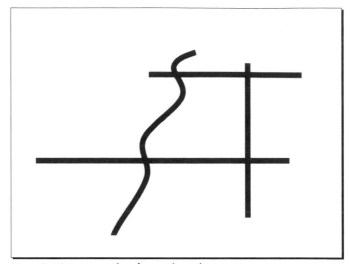

Figure 7-17: Intersecting lines forming the roads on a map

12. Click Line Style in the left pane and choose 8 from the Width drop-down menu.

13. Click Line and choose White from the Color pop-up menu to change the lines color to white.

14. Click Close.

15. Move the white lines to fit on top of the black 12-point lines by clicking and dragging or pressing the arrow keys (see Figure 7-18).

16. Import clip art or any images to enhance the appearance of your map by clicking the Insert tab and click the Clip Art tool. From the Clip Art task pane, select a clip art image.

For more information on working with clip art, see Chapter 9.

17. Click the Text Box button on the Insert tab and drag open a rectangle to create a text placeholder. Repeat, adding text placeholders as needed, and type the text to describe the street names (see Figure 7-18).

As an alternative to creating duplicate sets of lines, you can change the Format Shape of lines to a compound type of line style. Open the Format Shape dialog box after creating a line and click Line Style in the left pane. Open the Compound Type drop-down menu in the right pane and select a line style that appears similar to the lines drawn in this exercise. The advantage of this method is that you can create a map-type drawing much faster. The disadvantages are that you have no control over the line width on the edges, and you can't create intersections with the same appearances as described in the preceding steps.

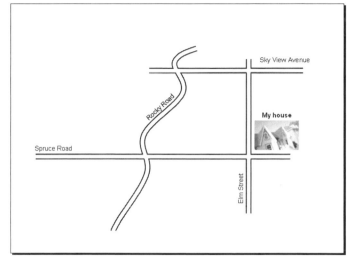

Figure 7-18: The finished map

Applying Themes and Styles

Color is an important element in communication. Each color has an inherent "personality" and can evoke emotion and action. Certain colors also have been historically associated with certain products, industries, and even messages. The colors you choose and the way you combine colors can have an effect on your presentation and how your audience perceives it. You want to ensure that your color choices are never arbitrary but, instead, are well thought-out.

Fortunately, PowerPoint makes choosing and using color simple. If you're not particularly color or graphically savvy, you can rest assured that PowerPoint's predefined themes are well designed. If you're feeling more creative, defining your own colors is easy. And if you decide color isn't enough, you also have the ability to add textures and patterns to your background and graphic elements. This chapter gives you the know-how to work with all three.

Chapter 8

Get ready to . . .

Apply a Theme

1. Open or create a new presentation in PowerPoint.

2. In the Ribbon, click the Design tab. In the Themes group, choose your desired theme, as shown in Figure 8-1. Hover your mouse over any theme to get a preview. Note that themes affect the formatting of colors, fonts, and effects of all elements on your slide.

3. To see more themes, click the More button. To see additional themes online, click the More button and then choose More Themes on Microsoft Office Online to download additional themes online.

4. When you apply a theme to a single blank slide in a new presentation, the theme for a title slide is applied. Add additional slides by clicking the Home tab in the Ribbon. In the Slides group, click New Slide and select your choice of slide types, as shown in Figure 8-2. Coordinated design variations of the theme are applied to your slide, depending on your slide type.

 The same themes are available in Word 2007 and Excel 2007, enabling you to keep all your documents and presentations consistent in look and feel.

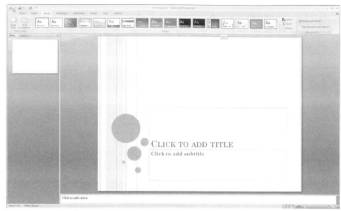

Figure 8-1: Apply a theme to your presentation

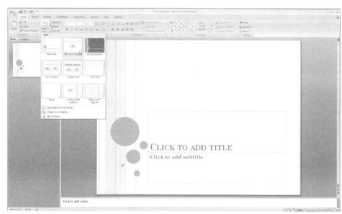

Figure 8-2: Add additional slides with design variations of the theme

Customize a Theme's Color

1. Open a presentation in PowerPoint.

2. In the Ribbon, click the Design tab. In the Themes group, click Theme Colors (or the Theme Colors button).

3. Choose your desired predefined color palette from the drop-down palette, as shown in Figure 8-3.

4. If you want to further customize your colors, choose Create New Theme Colors from the drop-down palette. In the Create New Theme Colors dialog box, select your desired colors for each of the 12 color "slots," as shown in Figure 8-4.

5. Name your customized color palette and click Save for use at a later date. Your saved theme now appears in the Themes gallery.

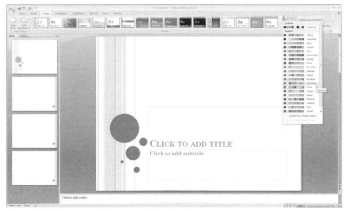

Figure 8-3: Choose a different predefined color palette

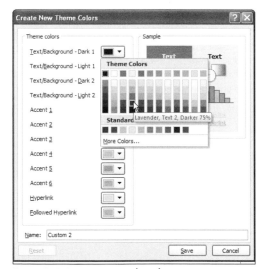

Figure 8-4: Customize your color palette

Customize a Theme's Fonts

1. Open a presentation in PowerPoint.

2. In the Ribbon, click the Design tab. In the Themes group, click Fonts.

3. Choose your desired font set from the drop-down list, as shown in Figure 8-5.

4. If you want to further customize your fonts, choose Create New Theme Fonts from the drop-down list. In the Create New Theme Fonts dialog box, choose your desired Heading and Body fonts from the drop-down lists.

5. Name your new font set and click Save, for use at a later date. Your saved theme now appears in the Themes gallery.

 Always make sure that both optimum readability and legibility are your prime considerations when choosing Fonts for your presentation. Note that fonts such as Georgia, Verdana, and Times New Roman were designed for best display on-screen.

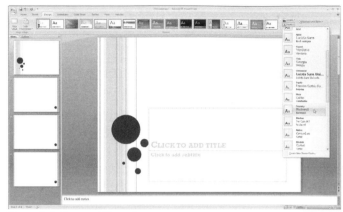

Figure 8-5: Choose a different font set

Choose a Theme's Effects

1. Open a presentation in PowerPoint.

2. In the Ribbon, click the Design tab. In the Themes group, click Effects.

3. Choose your desired effect from the drop-down list, as shown in Figure 8-6. Note that unlike colors and fonts, you can't create your own theme effects.

 You can apply effects to SmartArt graphics, shapes, pictures, WordArt, text, and tables.

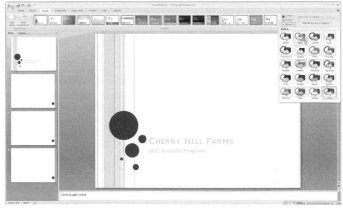

Figure 8-6: Choose an effect

Save a Customized Theme

1. Open a presentation in PowerPoint.

2. In the Ribbon, click the Design tab. Using the Themes group, customize your color and fonts as desired. Choose your theme's effect. Details on how to do so are provided in the section "Choose a Theme's Effects."

3. When you're done customizing your theme, click the Design tab in the Ribbon.

4. In the Themes group, click More and choose Save Current Theme.

5. Name the file and click Save. Your customized theme is added to the list of Custom Themes in the Themes gallery, as shown in Figure 8-7.

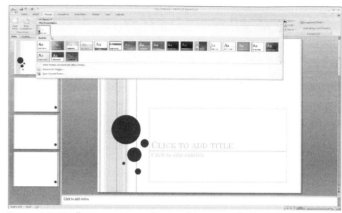

Figure 8-7: Totally customize your theme and then save it for later use.

Change a Slide Background Style

1. Open a presentation in PowerPoint and select your desired slides.

2. In the Ribbon, click the Design tab.

3. In the Background group, click Background Styles and select your desired predefined background style from the drop-down palette, as shown in Figure 8-8.

4. Choose whether to Apply To Selected Slides or Apply To All Slides. Note that if you have multiple slide masters in your presentation, you may choose to Apply To Matching Slides, which applies the new background to any slides that use the same slide master.

5. To further customize a background style, select your desired slides and in the Ribbon, click the Design tab. In the Background group, click the dialog box launcher (arrow) next to Background Styles. In the Format Background dialog box, choose your options for Fill and Picture, as shown in Figure 8-9. Feel free to select options to preview their appearance before you click Apply To All. If you want to go back to the original, click Reset Background.

 PowerPoint 2007 offers a background style, which includes two dark colors and two light colors that are used for text and the background. Each background also has three fill definitions: Subtle, Moderate, and Intense.

 To not display any graphics, choose Hide Background graphics.

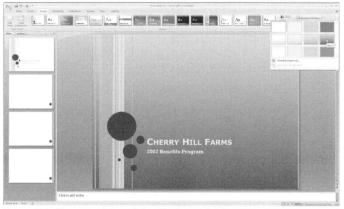

Figure 8-8: Choose another predefined background style

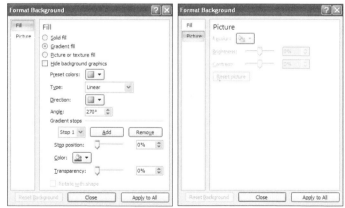

Figure 8-9: Customize a background style

Insert a Picture on a Slide Background

1. Open a presentation in PowerPoint and select your desired slides.

2. In the Ribbon, click the Design tab.

3. In the Background group, click the dialog box launcher (arrow) next to Background Styles. In the Format Background dialog box, select Fill tab and select Picture Or Texture Fill.

4. Click Insert From File and navigate to your desired photo, select it, and click Insert. Your picture fills the slide, as shown in Figure 8-10.

5. Click the Picture tab and make any needed color, brightness, and contrast adjustments.

Figure 8-10: Insert a picture on your background

Insert a Texture on a Slide Background

1. Open a presentation in PowerPoint and select your desired slides.

2. In the Ribbon, click the Design tab.

3. In the Background group, click the dialog box launcher (arrow) next to Background Styles. In the Format Background dialog box, select Fill tab and select Picture Or Texture Fill.

4. From the Texture drop-down palette, select your desired texture, as shown in Figure 8-11. Your texture fills the slide.

5. Click the Picture tab and make any needed color, brightness, and contrast adjustments.

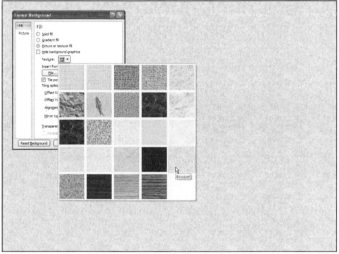

Figure 8-11: Insert a texture on your background

Insert a Solid or Gradient Fill on a Slide Background

1. Open a presentation in PowerPoint and select your desired slides.

2. In the Ribbon, click the Design tab.

3. In the Background group, click the dialog box launcher (arrow) next to Background Styles. In the Format Background dialog box, select Fill tab and select Solid Fill or Gradient Fill.

4. If you chose Solid Fill in Step 3, select your desired color from the drop-down palette, as shown in Figure 8-12. Adjust your transparency to your desired opaqueness.

5. If you chose Gradient in Step 3, specify your options, such as colors, gradient type, direction, angle, and transparency percentage, as shown in Figure 8-13. Note that *stops* refers to the particular colors that comprise the gradient.

6. Click Close to apply the solid color or gradient to the selected slide(s). Click Apply To All to apply the solid color or gradient to all of your slides.

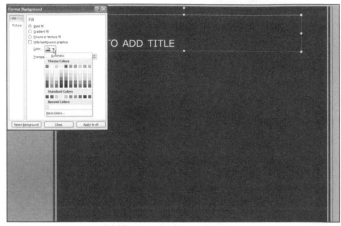

Figure 8-12: Insert a solid fill on your background

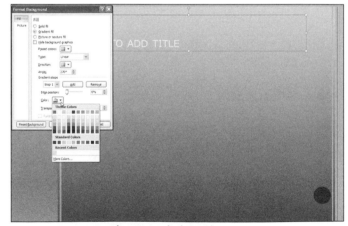

Figure 8-13: Insert a gradient on your background

Apply Quick Styles

1. Open a presentation in PowerPoint and select your desired slide.

2. Choose the element on your slide to which you want to apply a Quick Style.

3. In the Ribbon, click the Home tab and the <your element name>Tools tab.

4. In the Drawing group, click Quick Styles and choose your desired style from the drop-down palette, as shown in Figure 8-14. You find styles that include various colors, line styles, shadows, 3-D effects, gradients, and borders.

5. Note that Quick Styles also appears in the Ribbon with different names depending on what you're applying them to, as shown in Figure 8-15. Here's a quick guide to what they're called and where they're found in the Ribbon:

   • **For SmartArt graphics:** Design And SmartArt Tools, SmartArt Styles group

   • **Picture Styles:** Format And Picture Tools, Picture Styles group

   • **Shape Styles:** Format And Drawing Tools, Shapes Styles group

   • **WordArt Styles:** Format And Picture Tools, WordArt Styles group

   • **Text Styles:** Format And Drawing Tools, WordArt Styles group

 Quick Styles change how the colors, fonts, and effects are applied to your slide elements. They affect everything from tables and charts to SmartArt and shapes. Think of Quick Styles as going hand-in-hand with themes.

Figure 8-14: Apply a Quick Style

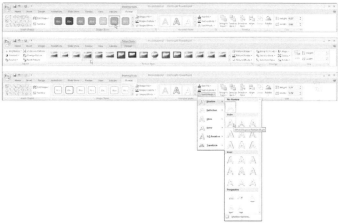

Figure 8-15: Names of Quick Styles change depending on the slide element selected

Change the Background of Notes or Handouts

1. Open a presentation in PowerPoint.

2. In the Ribbon, click the View tab.

3. In the Presentation Views group, click the Handouts or Notes Master.

4. In the Background group, click Background Styles.

5. Select your desired predefined background style, as shown in Figure 8-16.

6. To further fine-tune the background, click the dialog box launcher (arrow) next to Background Styles and choose Format Background from the drop-down palette.

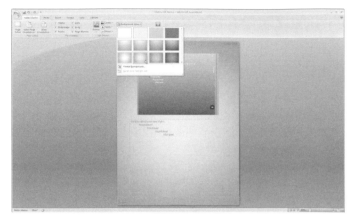

Figure 8-16: Choose a different background for Handouts or Notes

7. In the Format Background dialog box, select the Fill tab and specify your options as desired, as shown in Figure 8-17. Note that you may add a solid fill, gradient, picture, or texture. For details, see the sections in this chapter on applying these types of fills to backgrounds.

8. Note that you can change your Notes to grayscale or pure black and white. In the Color/Grayscale group, click the Grayscale or Pure Black And White buttons. Then choose your grayscale or black-and-white style in the Change Selected Object group, as shown in Figure 8-18.

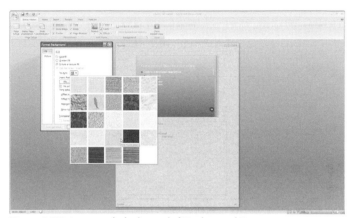

Figure 8-17: Customize the background of Handouts and Notes

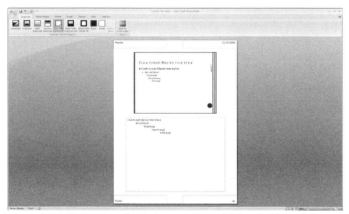

Figure 8-18: Convert your color Notes to grayscale or black and white

Working with Pictures

*T*he old adage, "A picture is worth a thousand words," is certainly true when it comes to presentations. Visually conveying information with images rather than words is often quicker, has more impact, and is more interesting.

Working with pictures in PowerPoint is easy. You can import a variety of file types, such as photos you've scanned or shot with your digital camera. You can also import clip art and photographs from stock agencies. Or you can just use the multitude of art available within PowerPoint's libraries, which include thousands pieces of clip art, photos, animations, and sounds. After you've chosen a picture, you can easily modify its size, position, and even contrast and color to suit your needs. This chapter gives you all the information necessary to work with pictures of all sorts.

Chapter 9

Get ready to . . .

Insert a Picture from Clip Art

1. Open a presentation in PowerPoint.

2. Click the slide where you want the clip art to appear.

3. In the Ribbon, click the Insert tab. In the Illustration group, click Clip Art. The Clip Art task pane appears.

4. In the Search For box, enter a keyword that describes the art you're looking for.

5. In the Search In box, select the collections from the drop-down list that you want PowerPoint to search in for your art. You can choose Everywhere (all collections), My Collections (clips you've stored on your hard drive), Office Collections (clips that are part of the Office suite), and Web Collections (clips located on the Web).

6. In the Results Should Be box, select your desired media type from the drop-down list. Choose from All Media Types, Clip Art, Photographs, Movies, and Sounds. For specific file formats under each media type, click the plus sign to expand the directory.

7. Click the Go button.

8. In the Results box, click the thumbnail of your desired clip. It is then inserted into your slide, as shown in Figure 9-1. To find similar clips (if the clip has a defined style), click the down arrow on the right of the clip and select Find Similar Style from the pop-up list. Note that you can also insert, copy, or delete clips from this pop-up list.

Figure 9-1: Insert clip art into your slide

 Click Organize Clips at the bottom of the Clip Art task pane to add, rearrange, or delete clips from your collections.

 For search keywords, you can also enter all or part of the filename of the art. If you don't know the exact name, you can use a question mark to substitute for a single character in a name or use an asterisk to substitute for multiple characters in the name. If you type two words, such as yellow leaves, in the Search For box, PowerPoint searches for clips using the keywords *yellow* and *leaves*. If you type two words enclosed by quotation marks, such as "yellow leaves," the program searches for clips that contain the phrase *yellow leaves*. And if you type in two words separated by a comma, such as yellow, leaves, PowerPoint searches for clips with the keywords *yellow* or *leaves*.

 The Clip Organizer holds your clips. Clips include clip art, photos, sounds, and videos. In addition to the Office clips that automatically reside in the Clip Organizer, you can access Office clips on the Web. You can also import and store your own clips in the Clip Organizer. Use this powerful tool to organize, find, and insert your clips.

Insert a Picture from a File

1. Open a presentation in PowerPoint.

2. Click the slide where you want the picture to appear. If you want the picture to appear on multiple slides or title slides, add it to the slide master or title master, respectively.

3. In the Ribbon, click the Insert tab. In the Illustration group, click Picture.

4. In the Insert Picture dialog box, navigate to your desired file. To add multiple pictures, press Ctrl as you click the pictures.

5. To embed the file into your PowerPoint presentation, choose Insert, as shown in Figure 9-2. To link the file to your PowerPoint presentation, click the down arrow next to Insert and choose Link To File. To do both, click the down arrow and choose Insert And Link.The picture is inserted into your slide, as shown in Figure 9-3.

 Embedded pictures become part of the presentation file. They don't change within the presentation file even if the picture is changed in its source program. Linked pictures do not become part of the presentation. The presentation only stores the location for the link and displays a *proxy* (a representation) of the picture. The picture will change within the presentation if it's modified in its source program.

 The From Scanner Or Camera option for adding pictures to a presentation is no longer available in PowerPoint 2007. You must first save your scanned images for download your digital photos to your computer. Then use the preceding steps to insert a picture from a file.

 To replace a picture, select it and in the Ribbon, click the Format within the Picture Tools tab. In the Adjust group, click Change Picture. Navigate to your desired new picture and double-click the image. You can also right-click the picture and choose Change Picture from the context menu.

Figure 9-2: Choose whether to embed or link your picture

Figure 9-3: A picture inserted into a slide

Insert a Picture from a Web Page

1. Open a presentation in PowerPoint.

2. Click the slide where you want the picture to appear.

3. On your Web page, right-click your desired picture and then choose Save Picture As from the context menu, as shown in Figure 9-4. Remember to make sure that you're not infringing on someone's copyright before you use it.

4. In the Save Picture dialog box, name your file and click Save. Remember where you saved your file.

5. In the Ribbon, click the Insert tab. In the Illustration group, click Picture.

6. In the Insert Picture dialog box, navigate to your saved picture and click Insert. The picture is inserted into your slide, as shown in Figure 9-5.

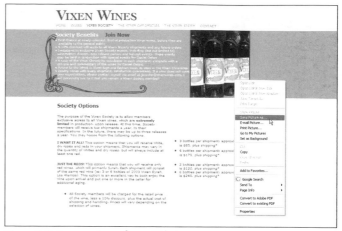

Figure 9-4: Copy your image from a Web site . . .

Figure 9-5: . . . and insert it into your presentation

Add a Clip to the Clip Organizer

1. Open a presentation in PowerPoint.

2. In the Ribbon, click the Insert tab. In the Illustration group, click Clip Art. The Clip Art task pane appears.

3. At the bottom of the Clip Art task pane, click the Organize Clips link, shown in Figure 9-6.

4. In the Microsoft Clip Organizer dialog box, choose File➪Add Clips To Organizer➪On My Own.

5. Locate and select the file you want to add.

6. Click Add To and select the collection you want to add the clip to, as shown in Figure 9-7. Click OK or click New to create a new collection.

7. Click Add. Close the Clip Organizer dialog box.

 You can also save pictures, WordArt, and shapes you created in PowerPoint. Select the object and choose Edit➪Copy. Select your desired collections folder and choose Edit➪Paste.

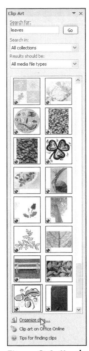

Figure 9-6: Use the Clip Organizer to store clips

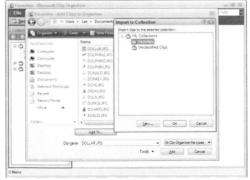

Figure 9-7: Store clips in the collection of your choice

Insert Pictures in a Photo Album

1. In the Ribbon, click the Insert tab. In the Illustrations group, click the arrow next to Photo Album and select New Photo Album to add a picture to a new photo album. Or select Edit Photo album to add a picture to an existing photo album.

2. In the Photo Album dialog box, click Insert Picture From File/Disk.

3. In the Insert New Pictures dialog box, navigate to and add the images you want in your album. You can insert pictures from files on your hard drive, as shown in Figure 9-8. You can also select multiple images at the same time. Click Insert.

4. To preview the image, make sure that it's selected in the Pictures In Album list. Rearrange the order of any of your photos and text boxes by clicking the up and down arrows directly under the Pictures In Album list.

5. You can also fix your images, as follows:

   • **Rotate:** Click the Rotate Left or Rotate Right buttons.

   • **Contrast:** Click the More Contrast or Less Contrast buttons.

   • **Brightness:** Click the More Brightness or Less Brightness buttons.

Figure 9-8: Insert images into your photo album

6. Choose your album layout. For example, you can choose to display 1, 2, or 4 pictures per slide. You can also choose the shape of your picture frame, such as a soft-edged rectangle, as shown in Figure 9-9.

7. You can also choose to apply a theme. Click the Browse button and choose your desired theme from the dialog box. For more on themes, see Chapter 8.

8. Click Create (if new) or Update (if existing). Your Photo Album appears, as shown in Figure 9-10.

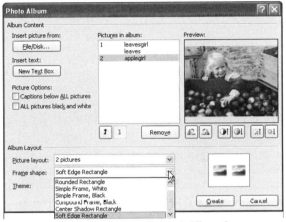

Figure 9-9: Customize your photo album with different frames

Figure 9-10: A photo album presentation

Resize a Picture Manually

1. Open a presentation in PowerPoint.

2. Select the picture you want to resize. You can also resize shapes, text boxes, and WordArt.

3. Position your mouse cursor over one of the handles surrounding the picture, as shown in Figure 9-11.

4. Drag the handle toward or away from the center to resize the picture smaller or larger. Remember to hold the Shift key down while you drag to keep the picture's original proportions. To keep the center of the object in the same place, press the Ctrl key while you drag.

Figure 9-11: Resize a picture by dragging a handle
Photo Credit: PhotoSpin

Resize a Picture Precisely

1. Open a presentation in PowerPoint.

2. Select the picture you want to resize. You can also resize shapes and WordArt.

3. In the Ribbon, click the Format/Picture Tools (or Drawing Tools for shapes and WordArt) tab. In the Size group, enter measurements in the Height and Width fields.

4. In the Size group, click the Dialog Box Launcher in the bottom right corner.

5. Click the Size tab in the Size And Position dialog box, shown in Figure 9-12.

6. Enter your desired size in the Height and Width boxes. Or enter your desired scale percentage in the Height and Width boxes.

7. Select the Lock Aspect Ratio option to keep the picture's original proportions.

 To resize SmartArt, select it and in the Ribbon, click the Format/SmartTools tab. Enter your desired Height and Width measurements.

Figure 9-12: Resize a picture by entering dimensions
Photo Credit: PhotoSpin

Crop a Picture

1. Open a presentation in PowerPoint.

2. Select the picture you want to crop.

    Cropping is one of the easiest things you can do to improve the composition of your pictures and home in on the focal point.

    Note that you can also "outcrop" a picture. Drag your cursor outward from your picture to add a margin around the image.

3. In the Ribbon, click the Format/Picture Tools tab. In the Size group, click Crop.

4. Position your cursor over a cropping handle and drag, as shown in Figure 9-13. To crop equally on two sides simultaneously, press the Ctrl key as you drag the center crop handle on a side. To crop equally on all four sides simultaneously, press the Ctrl key as you drag a corner crop handle.

5. Click anywhere in your slide outside the selected picture to deselect the Crop tool.

    To restore a picture to its original size, click the Format/Picture Tools tab in the Ribbon. In the Size group, click the Dialog Box Launcher in the bottom right corner. In the Size And Position dialog box, click the Size tab and uncheck the Lock Aspect Ratio option. Click Reset. But remember, you can't undo a crop if you compressed your image by selecting the Delete Cropped Areas Of Pictures option and either the Print or Screen output option.

Figure 9-13: Crop a picture
Photo Credit: PhotoSpin

Flip or Rotate a Picture

1. Open a presentation in PowerPoint.

2. Select the picture you want to flip or rotate. You can also flip or rotate shapes and WordArt.

3. In the Ribbon, click the Format/Picture Tools (Drawing Tools for shapes and WordArt) tab. In the Arrange group, click Rotate.

4. Select Rotate Right 90°, Rotate Left 90°, Flip Vertical, Flip Horizontal, or More Rotation Options, as shown in Figure 9-14.

5. If you selected More Rotation Options in Step 5, in the Size And Position dialog box, click the Size tab.

6. Enter your desired amount in the Rotation field.

 You can also manually rotate your picture. Simply drag the rotation handle (top center green circular handle) clockwise or counterclockwise.

Figure 9-14: Rotate or flip your pictures
Photo Credit: PhotoSpin

Align and Distribute Pictures

1. Open a presentation in PowerPoint.

2. Select the pictures you want to align. You can also align and distribute shapes and WordArt.

3. In the Ribbon, click the Format/Picture Tools (Drawing Tools for shapes and WordArt) tab. In the Arrange group, click Align.

4. You can align and distribute pictures relative to the slide or relative to each other. If you want to align and distribute relative to the slide, select the Align To Slide option first. Then click Align again and choose your alignment and distribution method, as shown in Figure 9-15.

5. Select your desired alignment or distribution method from the submenu. Note that the icons visually show each method.

Group Pictures

1. Open a presentation in PowerPoint.

2. Select the pictures you want to group. You can also group shapes and WordArt.

3. In the Ribbon, click the Format/Picture Tools (Drawing Tools for shapes and WordArt) tab. In the Arrange group, click Group.

4. Select Group from the drop-down list, as shown in Figure 9-16. Note that you can also ungroup pictures via this same drop-down list.

5. Your selected pictures are now grouped.

 If you have meticulously aligned and distributed numerous photos, you may want to group them to retain their precise alignment and spacing.

Figure 9-15: Align and distribute your pictures
Photo Credit: PhotoSpin

Figure 9-16: Group pictures to keep them together
Photo Credit: PhotoSpin

Adjust Picture Brightness and Contrast

1. Open a presentation in PowerPoint.

2. Select a picture that needs brightness or contrast adjustment.

3. In the Ribbon, click the Format/Picture Tools (Drawing Tools for shapes and WordArt) tab. In the Adjust group, click Brightness or Contrast.

4. Select your desired brightness or contrast percentage from the drop-down palette to adjust the brightness or contrast of the image.

5. To fine-tune your adjustment, click Picture Correction Options. In the Format Picture dialog box, drag the Brightness or Contrast slider right to lighten or increase contrast, and left to darken or decrease contrast.

6. Your picture's contrast and/or brightness is adjusted, as shown in Figure 9-17.

Figure 9-17: Adjust the brightness and contrast in a picture
Photo Credit: PhotoSpin

Recolor Pictures and Clip Art

1. Open a presentation in PowerPoint.

2. Select a picture that needs a color adjustment.

3. In the Ribbon, click the Format/Picture Tools tab.

4. In the Adjust group, click Recolor.

5. From the drop-down palette, choose from

   - **No Color:** Reverts the picture back to its default color

   - **Color Modes:** Choose from the following:

     Grayscale: Converts the picture to a grayscale image

     Sepia: Converts the picture to a brownish image, reminiscent of vintage photos

     Black And White: Converts the picture to a black-and-white image (two levels, either black or white)

     Washout: Desaturates the image

     Dark Variations: Colorizes the image with a hue and shade of black

     Light Variations: Colorizes the image with a hue and tint of white

     More Variations: Brings up a color palette where you can select your own color

6. Your picture's color is adjusted, as shown in Figure 9-18.

Want more control over editing your clip art? If you inserted a Windows Metafile (.wmf) from the Clipboard, first convert it into a drawing object by right-clicking the clip art and choosing Edit Picture. Click Yes in the dialog box. Use the tools in the Ribbon on the Format And Drawing Tools tab to modify the individual components of the clip art. Note that you can't modify bitmap files like JPEG, GIF, PNG, or TIFF, which can be modified only in an image-editing program.

Figure 9-18: Adjust the color of a picture
Photo Credit: PhotoSpin

Add Transparency to a Picture

1. Open a presentation in PowerPoint.

2. Select the picture you want to add transparency to. You can add transparency to bitmap images and some clip art.

3. In the Ribbon, click the Format/Picture Tools tab. In the Adjust group, click Recolor.

4. Select Set Transparent Color from the drop-down palette.

5. Within your picture, click the color you want to make transparent. That area becomes transparent, as shown in Figure 9-19.

 To undo any image adjustments (cropping, brightness and contrast, transparency, and so on), click the Format/Picture Tools tab in the Ribbon. In the Adjust group, click Reset Picture.

Figure 9-19: Add transparency to your pictures
Photo Credit: PhotoSpin

Compress a Picture to Reduce File Size

1. Open a presentation in PowerPoint.

2. Select the picture, or pictures, you want to compress.

3. In the Ribbon, click the Format/Picture Tools tab. In the Adjust group, click Compress Pictures.

4. In the Compress Pictures dialog box, select whether you want to apply the compression to selected pictures only. If you don't select this option, all your pictures will be compressed.

5. Next, click the Options button for different types or levels of compression, as shown in Figure 9-20:

   • **Automatically Perform Basic Compression On Save:** Compresses the picture information to create a smaller file when you save the file.

   • **Delete Cropped Areas Of Pictures:** Deletes areas of the pictures that were hidden during cropping.

   • **Target Output:** Choose the resolution that is appropriate for your desired medium — print, screen, or e-mail.

6. Click OK.

Figure 9-20: Compressing pictures makes file sizes smaller

 Compressing pictures shrinks their file sizes and allows them to download from the Web faster.

Add Effects

1. Open a presentation in PowerPoint.

2. Select the Shape(s), text, WordArt, clip art, or picture to which you want to add a shadow effect.

3. In the Ribbon, click the Format/Picture Tools tab. In the Picture Styles group, you can select one of the many preset styles, or . . .

4. In the Picture Styles group, click Picture Effects and choose your desired effect, such as shadow, glow, or bevel, from the drop-down palette. Your options vary according to the element you've selected.

5. Select the style of effect you want from the second flyout palette, as shown in Figure 9-21.

6. To change the specific settings of that effect, such as position or color, select <name of your effect> Options.

7. Your effect is applied, as shown in Figure 9-22. To remove the effect, select No <name of effect>.

 Note that when working with shapes, text or WordArt, menus will change to DrawingTools, Shape Styles, Shape Effects, WordArt Styles, and Text Effects.

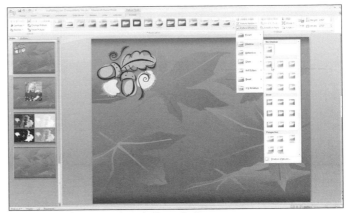

Figure 9-21: Choose your desired effect style

Figure 9-22: Effects can add additional interest to your art

Creating Tables and Charts

Data is often grasped more quickly and with more understanding and impact when it's presented in a simple, organized, and visual way. In PowerPoint, tables and charts are a couple of ways to effectively present data, especially quantitative, complex, or tedious data. This chapter describes the powerful options within PowerPoint to work with charts and tables. You can create tables and charts from scratch within PowerPoint or import them from Microsoft Word or Excel.

After you enter your data into a table or chart, PowerPoint provides the ability to change virtually all the elements, from modifying a table's font, columns and rows, borders, and shading to adding effects. You can even insert your favorite picture in a table cell. If you've created one of the many types of charts, PowerPoint provides the ability to alter almost all the chart objects by modifying a chart's type, font, axis, grid, borders, shading, labels, legend, and effects.

Get ready to . . .

Insert a Table

1. Open a presentation in PowerPoint.

2. In Normal view, under the Slides tab, select the slide on which you want to insert a table.

3. In the Ribbon, click the Insert tab. In the Tables group, click Table and do one of the following:

   • From the drop-down palette, move your mouse cursor to select your desired number of columns and rows for the table, as shown in Figure 10-1. Click OK.

   • Choose Insert Table and in the Insert Table dialog box, enter the number of columns and rows you desire, and click OK. Your table appears on the slide, as shown in Figure 10-2. To enter data, see "Enter Table Text in PowerPoint," later in this chapter.

Figure 10-1: Enter your desired number of table rows and columns

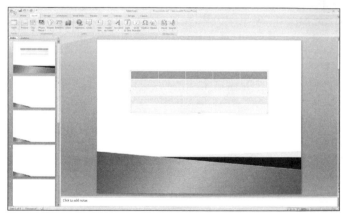

Figure 10-2: Your table appears on the slide

Insert a Table by Drawing

1. Open a presentation in PowerPoint.

2. In Normal view, under the Slides tab, select the slide on which you want to insert a table.

3. In the Ribbon, click the Insert tab. In the Tables group, click Table and choose Draw Table from the drop-down palette. The mouse cursor changes into a pencil icon.

4. To display a grid on the slide, click the View tab in the Ribbon and check Gridlines.

5. Click and drag diagonally across the table to define the outside border of the table. Release the mouse when you have your desired table shape, as shown in Figure 10-3.

6. To add columns or rows, click the Layout And Table Tools tab in the Ribbon.

7. In the Rows And Columns group, click Insert Above, Insert Below, Insert Right, or Insert Left. We added two additional rows, as shown in Figure 10-4. To add multiple rows or columns, select the number of rows or columns you want to add and then choose the appropriate Insert option. To enter data, see "Enter Table Text in PowerPoint," later in this chapter.

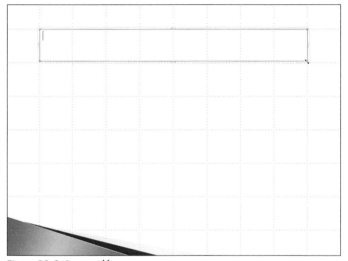

Figure 10-3: Draw a table

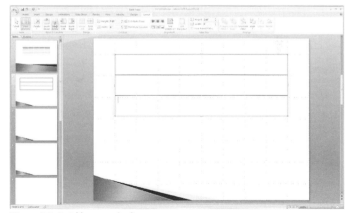

Figure 10-4: Add rows and columns

Copy a Table from Microsoft Word or Excel 2007

1. Open a presentation in PowerPoint.

2. In Normal view, under the Slides tab, select the slide on which you want to copy a table from Word or Excel.

3. Open Word, select your desired table, and in the Ribbon, click the Layout And Table Tools tab. In the Table group, click the arrow next to Table and choose Select Table from the drop-down list, as shown in Figure 10-5.

   In Excel, click the upper left cell of your table and drag diagonally to select the table.

4. In the Ribbon, click the Home tab; in the Clipboard group, click Copy. Note that you can also right-click anywhere within the selection of cells and choose Copy from the context menu.

5. In PowerPoint, in the Ribbon, click the Home tab; in the Clipboard group, click Paste. Your table is inserted on the slide.

6. Resize the table by dragging a corner sizing handle; click and drag the table to reposition it. To enter or format data, see "Enter Table Text in PowerPoint," or "Format Table Text," later in this chapter. Our sized and formatted slide appears in Figure 10-6.

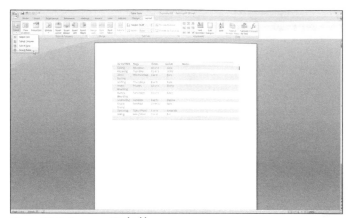

Figure 10-5: Copy your Word table

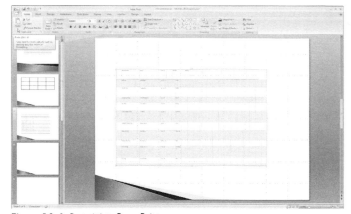

Figure 10-6: Paste it into PowerPoint

Insert a Table from Microsoft Excel 2007

1. Open a presentation in PowerPoint.

2. In Normal view, under the Slides tab, select the slide on which you want to insert a table from Excel.

3. In the Ribbon, click the Insert tab. In the Table group, click Table and choose Excel Spreadsheet from the drop-down palette. Your table is inserted on the slide, as shown in Figure 10-7.

4. Click in a cell and enter your data as desired. Resize the table by dragging a corner sizing handle; click and drag the table to reposition it.

 When you insert a table from Excel, you're embedding it as an OLE object so that you can benefit from the added functionality of Excel tables (such as calculation capabilities), but you're limited in formatting the table in PowerPoint.

Figure 10-7: Insert a table from Excel 2007

Enter Table Text in PowerPoint

1. Open a presentation in PowerPoint.

2. In Normal view, under the Slides tab, select the slide that contains the table where you want to enter text.

3. Click within a cell and type your desired text, as shown in Figure 10-8. If you type to the end of the cell, the text automatically wraps to the next line.

4. Press Tab to advance to the next cell to the right. If you're at the end of the row, you advance to the first cell in the next row.

5. Press Enter to insert another line within a cell.

6. Press Ctrl+Tab to insert a tab within a cell. After you've entered your text, click outside the table.

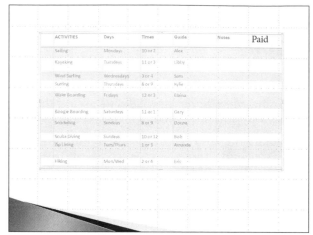

Figure 10-8: Insert table text

 Note that if you want to enter an equation and you don't want to use Excel, you can create a SmartArt graphic (in the Process category). For more on SmartArt graphics, see Chapter 11.

 Press the up-arrow or down-arrow key to move up or down in a column. Press the left and right arrows to move side to side within the table.

Format Table Text

1. Open a presentation in PowerPoint.

2. In Normal view, under the Slides tab, select the slide that contains the table you want to format.

3. Highlight your text within the cell, row, or column.

4. In the Ribbon, click the Home tab. In the Font group, choose your desired font attributes, as shown in Figure 10-9.

5. To format text alignment, in the Ribbon, click the alignment buttons in the Paragraph group. You can also click the Layout tab and in the Alignment group, click the buttons to align text left, center, or right. You can also align text to the top, bottom, or center of the cells.

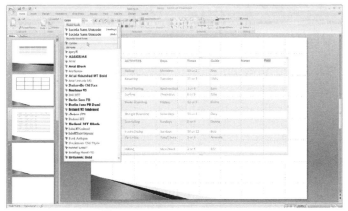

Figure 10-9: Format table text

 You can also specify the margins of the table cells. Select your desired cells or the entire table and then click Cells in the Alignment group and choose your desired options to add space around the content within the cell.

Add and Modify Table Columns and Rows

1. Open a presentation in PowerPoint.

2. In Normal view, under the Slides tab, select the slide that contains the table you want to modify.

3. Select the table, and in the Ribbon, click the Layout tab.

4. To add a row, click in the row above or below where the new row is to be inserted.

5. In the Rows And Columns group, click Insert Above or Insert Below. To add multiple rows, select the number of rows you want to add within the displayed table and then choose your Insert option. The same number of selected rows is inserted while the selected cells move above or below them, depending on your Insert selection.

6. To add a column, click in the column to the right or left where the new column is to be inserted.

7. In the Rows And Columns group, click Insert Right or Insert Left. We added a column to the right, as shown in Figure 10-10. To add multiple columns, select the number of columns you want to add and then choose your Insert option. A table with added rows and columns appears in Figure 10-11.

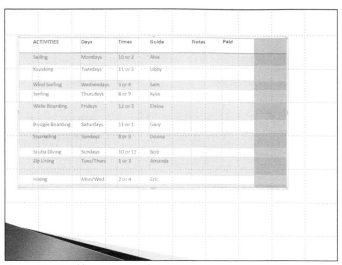

Figure 10-10: Add a new row or column

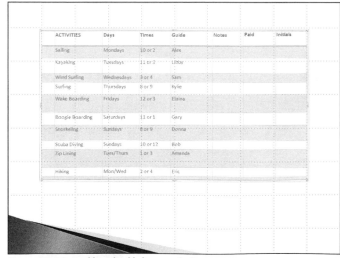

Figure 10-11: A table with added rows and columns

You can also click the row or column next to the point where you want to insert a new one. Then right-click and choose Insert Rows Above, Insert Rows Below, Insert Columns To The Right, and Insert Columns To The Left from the context menu, as shown in Figure 10-12.

8. To change the size of any row, first click outside the table to deselect any cells.

9. Position the pointer on the lower border of the row to be modified. Your cursor changes to a double-headed arrow, as shown in Figure 10-13.

10. Click and drag the border up or down to increase or decrease the height.

 To change the height of all rows evenly, click anywhere on the table to select it. In the Ribbon, under the Layout And Table Tools tab, click Distribute Rows. The rows are set to the same height, and the content adjusts to fit.

11. To change the width of any column, first click outside the table to deselect any cells.

12. Position the pointer on the right border of the column to be modified. With the double-headed arrow cursor, click and drag the border to the left or right to increase or decrease the width.

 To change the size of all columns evenly, click anywhere on the table to select it and then in the Ribbon under the Layout And Table Tools tab, click Distribute Columns Evenly. The columns are set to the same width, and the content adjusts to fit.

Figure 10-12: Add rows and columns via the context menu

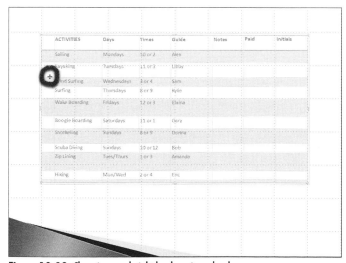

Figure 10-13: Changing row height by dragging a border

Merge and Split Cells

1. Open a presentation in PowerPoint.

2. In Normal view, under the Slides tab, select the slide that contains the table you want to modify.

3. To merge (combine) cells in your table, do one of the following:

   - Select the cells you want to merge. Note that they must be adjacent to one another. In the Ribbon, click the Layout tab. In the Merge group, choose Merge Cells, as shown in Figure 10-14.

   - In the Ribbon, click the Design tab. In the Draw Borders group, click Eraser. Select the cell borders you want to erase. When done, press the Esc button.

4. To split a cell in your table, select your desired cell.

5. In the Ribbon, click the Layout And Table Tools tab. In the Merge group, click Split Cells and then do one of the following, as shown in Figure 10-15.

   - To divide the cell vertically, enter the number of cells you want in the Number Of Columns field.

   - To divide the cell horizontally, enter the number of cells you want in the Number Of Rows field.

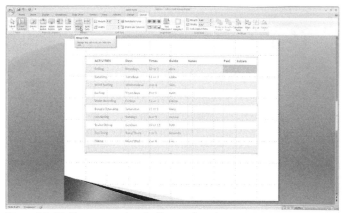

Figure 10-14: Merge your selected cells to combine them

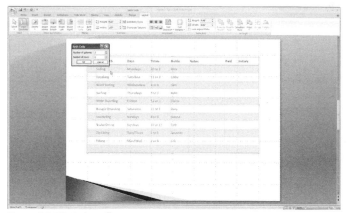

Figure 10-15: Spilt a cell into two

Modify a Table's Style

1. Open a presentation in PowerPoint.

2. In Normal view, under the Slides tab, select the slide that contains the table you want to modify.

3. Click the edge of the table to select the entire table. Note that if you click inside a cell, only the cell borders will be formatted.

4. In the Ribbon, click the Design tab.

5. In the Table Styles group, select your desired style. Click More options to view additional styles, as shown in Figure 10-16.

6. Under table Quick Style Options, you can add additional options, such as Banded Rows, a Header Row, and First Column, as shown in Figure 10-17.

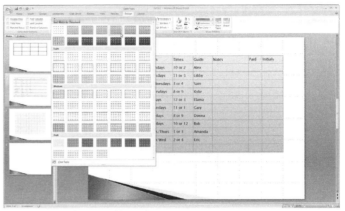

Figure 10-16: Change a table's style

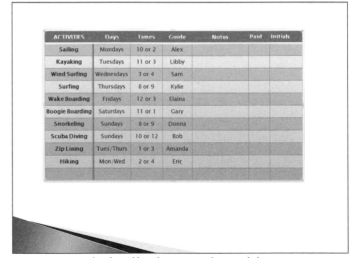

Figure 10-17: Apply other table style options, such as Banded Rows

Apply Shading or Border to Table Elements

1. Open a presentation in PowerPoint.

2. In Normal view, under the Slides tab, select the slide that contains the table you want to modify.

3. Select the entire table by clicking the edge of the table. To select a single cell, simply click inside that cell. To select a group of cells, drag your cursor through your desired cells.

4. In the Ribbon, click the Design tab and in the Table Styles group, click Shading (represented by the button with the paint bucket) and select your desired color from the drop-down palette.

5. To apply a border, click the arrow next to Borders and select your desired border from the drop-down list, as shown in Figure 10-18.

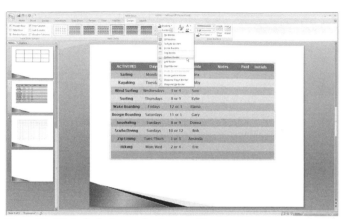

Figure 10-18: Apply shading or a border to a table

Apply Effects to Table Elements

1. Open a presentation in PowerPoint.

2. In Normal view, under the Slides tab, select the slide that contains the table you want to add an effect to.

3. Select the table, row, column, or cell to which you want to apply the fill effect.

4. In the Ribbon, click the Design tab, click Effects, and select your desired effect from the drop-down list. Next select your effect style from the second drop-down list, as shown in Figure 10-19.

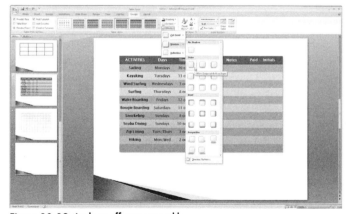

Figure 10-19: Apply an effect to your table

Insert Pictures into a Table

1. Open a presentation in PowerPoint.

2. In Normal view, under the Slides tab, select the slide that contains the table you want to insert a picture into.

3. Select the table, row, column, or cell into which you want to insert a picture.

4. In the Ribbon, click the Design tab. In the Table Styles group, click Shading and then choose Picture from the drop-down palette, as shown in Figure 10-20.

5. In the Insert Picture dialog box, navigate to your desired image, select it, and click Insert. The picture appears in your table, as shown in Figure 10-21.

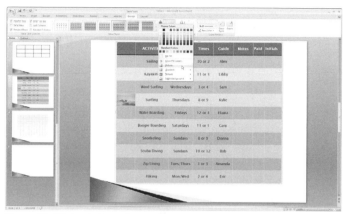

Figure 10-20: Insert pictures into a table

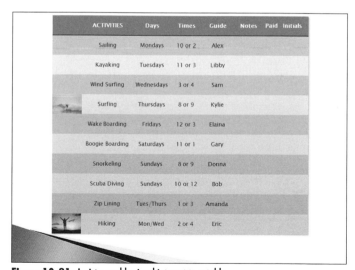

Figure 10-21: A picture adds visual interest to a table
Photo Credit: PhotoSpin

Insert and Embed a Chart

1. Open a presentation in PowerPoint.

2. In Normal view, under the Slides tab, select the slide on which you want to insert a graph.

3. In the Ribbon, click the Insert tab. In the Illustrations group, click Chart.

4. In the Insert Chart dialog box, select the type of chart on the left and then the style of that type on the right. Click OK.

5. Excel 2007 opens a worksheet with sample data. Click in the cells and enter your own data and labels, as shown in Figure 10-22.

6. In the Ribbon, click the Microsoft Office button and choose Save As. In the Save As dialog box, choose your desired folder or drive from the Save in list. Name the file and click Save.

7. In the Ribbon, click the Microsoft Office button and choose Close.

8. Return to PowerPoint where your chart appears on the slide, as shown in Figure 10-23.

 Use the sizing handles to resize the graph. Drag to reposition the chart.

 If you do not have Excel 2007 installed, when you create a new chart, Microsoft Graph opens along with a chart and datasheet. Enter data in the datasheet and create the chart.

Figure 10-22: Enter data in the Excel worksheet

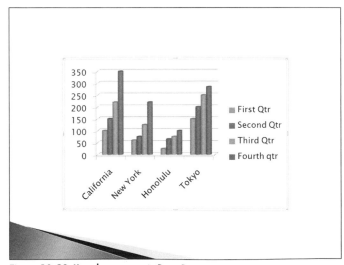

Figure 10-23: Your chart appears in PowerPoint

Paste an Excel Chart

1. Open Excel and select the chart you want to insert.

2. In the Ribbon, click the Home tab.

3. In the Clipboard group, choose Cut, as shown in Figure 10-24.

4. Return to PowerPoint and select the slide on which you want to paste the chart.

5. In the Ribbon, click the Home tab.

6. In the Clipboard group, click the arrow under Paste and choose Paste Special. In the Paste Special dialog box, choose either Paste or Paste Link (see tip below). The Excel chart is pasted onto the slide, as shown in Figure 10-25.

When you choose Paste Link in Step 6, your chart is linked to the data in your Excel worksheet. When you update the worksheet, the chart is updated as well.

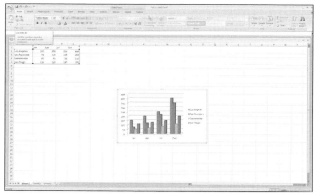

Figure 10-24: Cut your chart in Excel

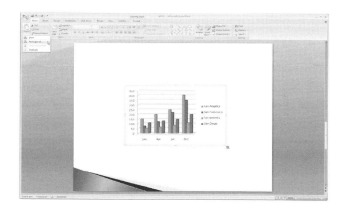

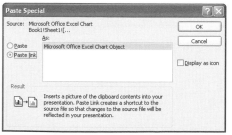

Figure 10-25: Paste your Excel chart in PowerPoint

Edit the Chart's Data

1. Open a presentation in PowerPoint.

2. In Normal view, under the Slides tab, select the slide containing the chart you want to edit.

3. In the Ribbon, click the Design tab.

4. Choose Edit Data in the Data group.

5. The Excel spreadsheet appears. Modify your data as desired.

6. In the Ribbon, click the MS Office button and choose Close.

7. Return to PowerPoint. Your chart is dynamically updated, as shown in Figure 10-26.

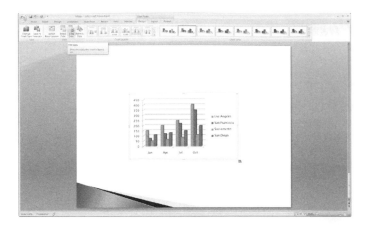

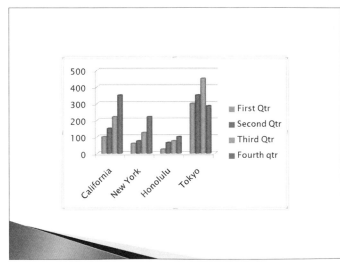

Figure 10-26: Edit your chart's data

Change a Chart's Type

1. Open a presentation in PowerPoint.

2. In Normal view, under the Slides tab, select the slide containing the chart to be modified.

3. In the Ribbon, click the Design tab. In the Type group, click Change Chart Type.

4. In the Chart Type dialog box, shown in Figure 10-27, select your desired type from the Chart type list and then select your desired type style from the Chart palette on the right.

5. To finish, click OK. Your modified chart appears.

Select Chart Elements Efficiently

1. Open a presentation in PowerPoint.

2. In Normal view, under the Slides tab, select the slide containing your desired chart.

3. In the Ribbon, click the Layout tab.

4. In the Current Selection group, choose your desired chart element(s) from the drop-down list, as shown in Figure 10-28.

5. You can then format the layout or design of those selected elements. To reset your chart to its original visual style, click the Reset To Match Style button in the Ribbon.

 Your chart consists of several components that are enclosed within the chart area, as indicated by the border that appears when you select the chart. The area that contains your axes, values, grid lines, and symbols such as bars, pie, and lines (depending on your chart type) is referred to as the *plot area*. The *legend area* explains the symbols used in the chart. To find out what other individual chart components are called, simply hover your mouse over the item to view a description.

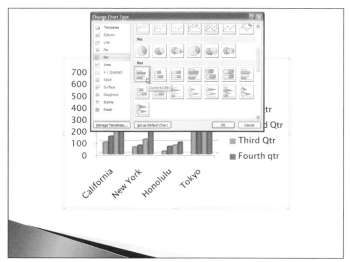

Figure 10-27: Change a chart type

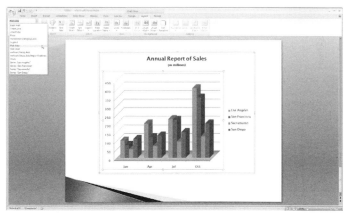

Figure 10-28: Select your chart elements

Change a Chart's Style or Layout

1. Open a presentation in PowerPoint.

2. In Normal view, under the Slides tab, select the slide containing your desired chart.

3. In the Ribbon, click the Design tab.

4. In the Chart Styles group, choose your desired chart style. Changing the chart style essentially changes the colors of the chart, as shown in Figure 10-29.

5. To change a chart's layout, click the More arrow in the Chart Layouts group. Choose your desired layout, as shown in Figure 10-30.

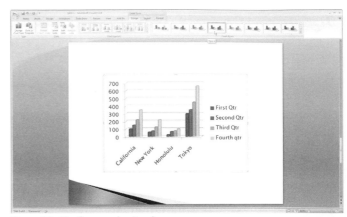

Figure 10-29: Change a chart's style

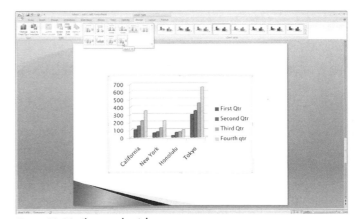

Figure 10-30: Change a chart's layout

Format a Graph's Text

1. Open a presentation in PowerPoint.

2. In Normal view, under the Slides tab, select the slide that contains the chart with the text to be formatted.

3. Select the text box.

4. In the Ribbon, click the Home tab.

5. In the Font group, modify the font type, size, color, and style, as shown in Figure 10-31.

6. Click OK.

 To change other attributes, such as the outline or effects of the type, click the Format And Chart Tools tab in the Ribbon and in the WordArt Styles group and make your modifications, as shown in Figure 10-32.

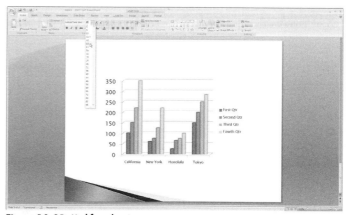

Figure 10-31: Modify a chart's text

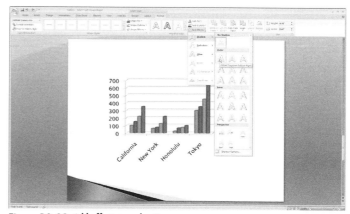

Figure 10-32: Add effects to a chart's text

Format a Chart's Legend and Titles

1. Open a presentation in PowerPoint.

2. In Normal view, under the Slides tab, select the slide that contains the chart to be modified.

3. In the Ribbon, click the Layout tab.

4. In the Labels group, click Legend and from the drop-down list, choose your desired legend option. Note that the thumbnails give you a visual representation of the legend's placement.

5. To format the titles in the axes, in the Labels group, click Axis Titles and choose either Primary Horizontal Axis Title or Primary Vertical Axis Title. Then from the submenu, choose your desired position of the horizontal or vertical axis title, as shown in Figure 10-33.

6. To format the chart title, in the Labels group, click Chart Title and choose your desired style of title. Choose More Options to access other attributes, such as Fill, Border Color, Border Styles, Shadow, and so on, as shown in Figure 10-34.

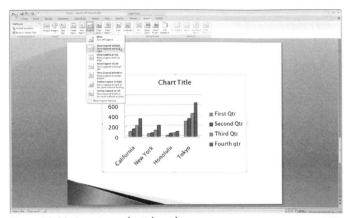

Figure 10-33: Format your chart's legend

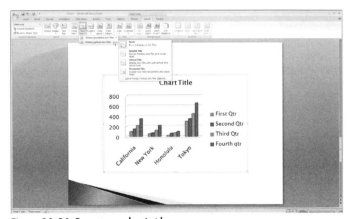

Figure 10-34: Format your chart's titles

Format a Chart's Data Labels

1. Open a presentation in PowerPoint.

2. In Normal view, under the Slides tab, select the slide that contains the chart to be modified.

3. In the Ribbon, click the Layout tab.

4. In the Labels group, click Data Labels and choose whether you want the labels to be displayed or turned off, as shown in Figure 10-35. Labels are applied to each of your data points.

5. To access more options, choose More Data Label Options.

6. Under Label Options, choose whether you want your label to include the series of category names or just the value. Note that you can check each option to preview how it will appear on your chart. You can also format the type of Number (for example, currency or percentage).

7. Finally, you can format other options, such as type of Fill, Border Color and Styles, Shadow, 3-D Format, and Alignment.

Format a Chart's Axes

1. Open a presentation in PowerPoint.

2. In Normal view, under the Slides tab, select the slide that contains the chart to be modified.

3. In the Ribbon, click the Layout tab.

4. In the Axes group, choose Primary Horizontal or Primary Vertical Axis.

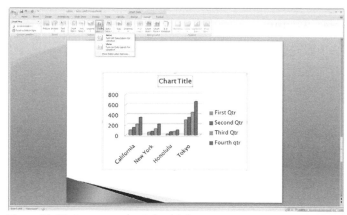

Figure 10-35: Format your chart's data labels

5. For Primary Horizontal Axis, from the submenu, choose whether you want to show no axis, a default axis, a left-to-right axis, show an axis without labels or tick marks, or show a right-to-left axis.

6. For Primary Vertical Axis, from the submenu, choose whether you want to show no axis, a default axis, or an axis in units of thousands, millions, or billions, or a 10 based log scale, as shown in Figure 10-36.

7. You can also access More Primary Vertical Axis Options to format attributes such as the type of tick marks and the minimum and maximum values of the scale of your axis. Likewise, you can access additional More Primary Horizontal Axis Options.

8. Other options include the formatting of your numbers and the type of Fill, Line Color and Style, Shadow 3-D Format, and Alignment.

Format Gridlines

1. Open a presentation in PowerPoint.

2. In Normal view, under the Slides tab, select the slide that contains the chart to be modified.

3. In the Ribbon, click the Layout tab.

4. In the Axes group, choose Gridlines and choose either Primary Horizontal Gridlines or Primary Vertical Gridlines.

5. From the submenu choose either None, Major Gridlines, Minor Gridlines, or Major and Minor Gridlines, as shown in Figure 10-37.

6. You can also access More Primary Vertical (or Horizontal) Gridlines to format attributes such as Line Color and Style and Shadow.

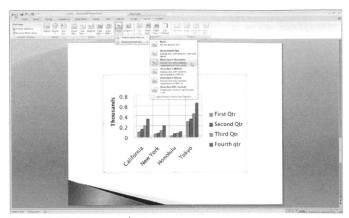

Figure 10-36: Format your chart's axes

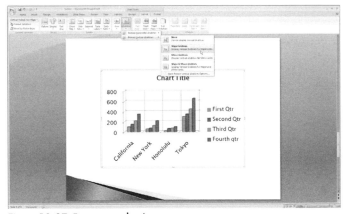

Figure 10-37: Format your chart's axes

Format a Chart's Background

1. Open a presentation in PowerPoint.

2. In Normal view, under the Slides tab, select the slide that contains the chart to be modified.

3. In the Ribbon, click the Layout tab.

4. In the Background group, you can format the following:

   • **Plot Area:** Format the plot area, which includes everything but the legend and titles

   • **Chart Wall:** Format whether you show the chart's wall and, if so, you can choose More Options to further format the Fill, Border Color and Style, Shadow, 3-D Format, and Rotation.

   • **Chart Floor:** Format whether you show the chart's floor and, if so, you can choose More Options to further format the Fill, Border Color and Style, Shadow, 3-D Format, and Rotation.

   • **3-D Rotation:** For 3-D Charts, you can alter the degrees of rotation, as shown in Figure 10-38. Figure 10-39 shows a fully formatted chart

Figure 10-38: Change the rotation of a 3-D chart

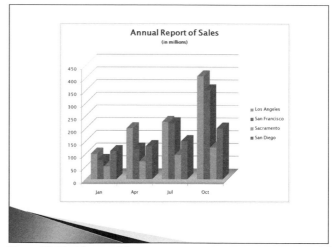

Figure 10-39: A formatted chart

Insert a Picture into a Chart

1. Open a presentation in PowerPoint.

2. In Normal view, under the Slides tab, select the slide that contains the chart on which you want to insert a picture.

3. In the Insert Picture dialog box, navigate to your desired image, select it, and click Insert.

4. Size the photo to fit as desired by dragging a corner handle. Figure 10-40 shows an inserted and sized picture. Note that your nicely inserted picture isn't actually part of the table. If you move your table, the picture remains where it is. For more details on working with pictures, see Chapter 9.

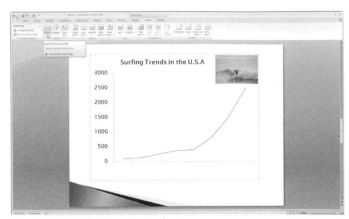

Figure 10-40: Add a picture to your chart

Creating Organizational Charts and Diagrams using SmartArt

Sometimes, trying to figure out who reports to whom and who is responsible for what area can be downright confusing, especially in large corporations with multiple divisions, locations, and product lines. Rather than using running lists of people's names, titles, and responsibilities, it's more effective to use organizational charts. *Org charts*, as they're called in corporate circles, graphically display how a corporate hierarchy is structured. Viewers can quickly see how the company is organized — either by personnel, by function, by product, or by location. Not the corporate type? Well, organizational-type charts can also be used to display family trees, biological classifications, and other types of hierarchical information. Similarly, diagrams also offer a visual solution to presenting complicated data, especially data such as processes, workflow, relationships, and causes and effects.

Like tables and graphs, organization charts and diagrams provide important but complex and sometimes tedious information visually, making it easier and quicker for the viewer to comprehend. And with Microsoft Office 2007's new SmartArt feature, creating these charts and diagrams has never been easier. This chapter covers everything you need to know to create both effective and attractive org charts and diagrams.

Chapter 11

Get ready to . . .

Creating SmartArt Graphics

1. Open a presentation in PowerPoint. Navigate to the slide on which you want to put your SmartArt.

2. In the Ribbon, click the Insert tab. In the Illustrations group, click SmartArt.

3. In the Choose A SmartArt Graphic dialog box, select your type of graphic from the list at the left. Then choose your desired layout for that type, shown in Figure 11-1. Click OK. Your SmartArt graphic appears on your slide.

4. To add text to the graphic, click inside the Text placeholder and type. If there is no Text placeholder, simply click in the shape and type. You can also enter your text in the Text pane. Click the Text pane button in the Ribbon and enter your text in the pane. A SmartArt graphic appears, as shown in Figure 11-2.

 SmartArt, new to PowerPoint 2007, enables you to easily create and edit various types of information graphics that show process, relationships, hierarchy, and so on. You can create everything from organization charts and cycle diagrams to flowcharts and pyramids. Be sure to choose the type of SmartArt that will best present your data. Note that you can also create SmartArt graphics in Word and Excel 2007.

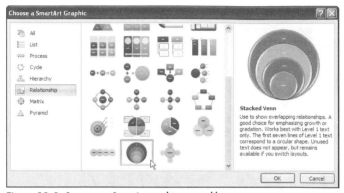

Figure 11-1: Create your SmartArt graphic type and layout

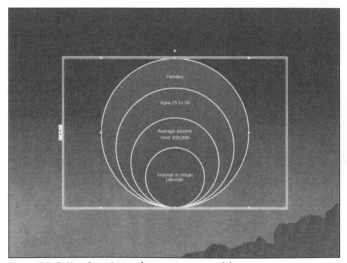

Figure 11-2: Your SmartArt graphic appears on your slide

Add and Delete Shapes in a SmartArt Graphic

1. Open a presentation in PowerPoint.

2. Select your organization chart. Then select the existing shape to which you want to add a shape.

3. In the Ribbon, click the Design/SmartArt Tools tab.

4. In the Create Graphic group, click the arrow under Add Shape and choose an option from the submenu, shown in Figure 11-3.

5. To delete a shape, click its border and press Delete.

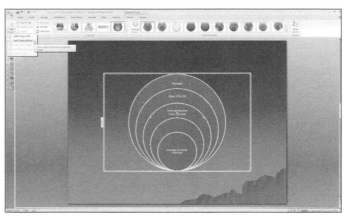

Figure 11-3: Add shapes to a SmartArt graphic

Convert a SmartArt Graphic Type or Layout

1. Open a presentation in PowerPoint.

2. To convert your SmartArt Graphic to another type or layout, select the diagram, and in the Ribbon, click the Design/SmartArt Tools tab.

3. To change the type, in the Layout Group, click the More button, just to the right of the visible layout thumbnails. Select your desired type and layout from the Choose SmartArt Graphic dialog box. Note that after converting to another type, shown in Figure 11-4, you may have to rearrange the elements in your diagram, as well as modify your text attributes.

4. To change the layout, in the Layout Group, select your new layout. To access additional layout styles, click the More button, just to the right of the visible layout thumbnails.

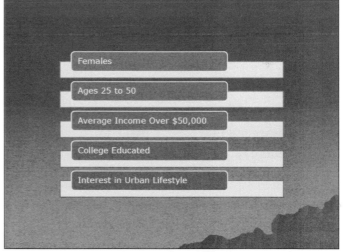

Figure 11-4: Convert your SmartArt graphic to a different type

Format and Edit SmartArt Graphics

1. You can easily customize your SmartArt graphic by selecting your graphic and doing any or all of the following:

   - **Change colors:** In the Ribbon, click the Design And SmartArt Tools tab. In the SmartArt Styles group, click Change Colors and choose your color variation.

   - **Apply a SmartArt Style:** In the Ribbon, click the Design And SmartArt Tools tab. In the SmartArt Styles group, select your desired SmartArt style. Click the More button to the right of the style thumbnails to view additional styles. Note that if you hover your mouse over the style, you see a preview of that style.

   - **Move your shape:** Select and drag your shape to a new location on the chart.

   - **Choose a different shape:** Click the Format tab and in the Shapes group, choose Change Shape and choose a different shape from the drop-down palette.

   - **Resize your shape:** Click the Format tab and in the Shapes group, choose Larger or Smaller to size your shape. You can also place your mouse cursor over a corner and drag to your desired size.

   - **Choose a different shape outline style:** Click the Format tab and in the Shapes Styles group, select a different shape outline style. Hover your mouse button over a style to preview it.

   - **Choose a different shape color:** Click the Format tab and in the Shapes Styles group, choose Shape Fill and choose a different color for your shape, as shown in Figure 11-5. You can also choose a gradient or even a photo for your shape.

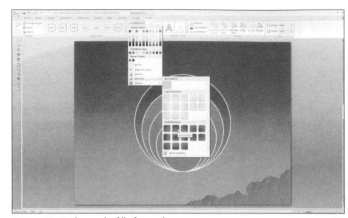

Figure 11-5: Change the fill of your shape

- **Choose a different shape line:** Click the Format tab and in the Shapes Styles group, choose Shape Outline and choose a different color, line weight or line style (for example, dashed) for your shape.

- **Choose a different shape effect:** Click the Format tab and in the Shapes Styles group, choose Shape Effects and choose a different effect, such as a shadow, glow, or bevel for your shape.

- **Choose different font attributes:** Click the Home tab and in the Font group, change the font size, style, or color of the text in a shape.

- **Choose different WordArt attributes:** Click the Format tab and in the WordArt group, change the text fill, text outline, and text effects of the text in a shape.

A customized SmartArt graphic appears in Figure 11-6.

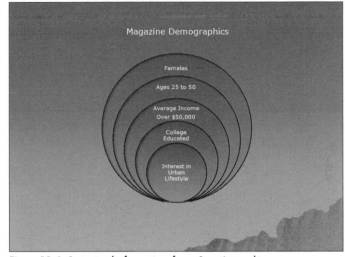

Figure 11-6: Customize the formatting of your SmartArt graphic

Create an Organization Chart

1. Open a presentation in PowerPoint. Navigate to the slide on which you want to put your org chart.

2. In the Ribbon, click the Insert tab. In the Illustrations group, click SmartArt.

3. In the Choose SmartArt Graphic dialog box, from the list of types on the left, click Hierarchy.

4. Choose the Organization Chart layout and click OK, as shown in Figure 11-7. Your basic organization chart appears on your slide.

5. To add text to the chart, click in the Text placeholder and type. You can also enter your text in the Text pane. Click the Text pane button in the Ribbon (or click the arrows on the left of the chart bounding box) and enter your text in the pane, as shown in Figure 11-8.

 To manually modify the size of the diagram, select the chart and drag the corner sizing handle on the border, which proportionally resizes the chart.

 Although using SmartArt is the preferred method, you can also create an organization chart using the Organization Chart Add-in. Make sure that the Add-in is installed before you start. Installation depends on your operating system. For instructions, type "Where Can I find Microsoft Office Organization Chart Add-in" in the PowerPoint Help search field. Once installed, click the Insert tab in the Ribbon. Then in the Text Group, click Object and in the Insert Object dialog box, choose Organization Chart Add-in from the Object Type list. To add boxes, click the button for your desired box type. To add text, click inside a box. When done, choose File⟶Close & Return To [filename].

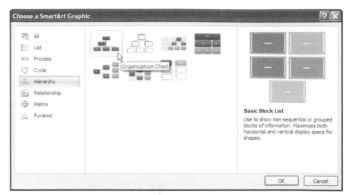

Figure 11-7: Insert an organization chart

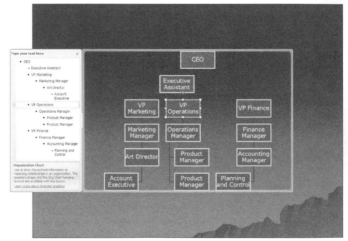

Figure 11-8: Enter the text for your chart boxes

Add and Delete Shapes in an Organization Chart

1. Open a presentation in PowerPoint.

2. Select your organization chart. Then select the existing shape that you want to add to.

3. In the Ribbon, click the Design/SmartArt Tools tab.

4. In the Create Graphic group, click the arrow under Add Shape and choose one of the following from the sub-menu, as shown in Figure 11-9:

   - **Add Shape After:** Adds a shape at the same level after the existing shape.

   - **Add Shape Before:** Adds a shape at the same level before the existing shape.

   - **Add Shape Above:** Adds a shape one level above the existing shape.

   - **Add Shape Below:** Adds a shape one level below the existing shape.

   - **Add Assistant:** Adds a shape between the existing shape and any shapes below the existing shape.

5. To delete a shape, click its border and press Delete.

6. To add text to a shape, simply click in the shape and type.

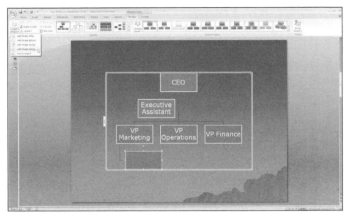

Figure 11-9: Add shapes to your org chart

Modify an Organization Chart Style

1. Open a presentation in PowerPoint.

2. To modify the overall style of the organization chart, select the chart and in the Ribbon, click the Design tab.

3. In the SmartArt Styles group, choose your desired style. We chose the Intense Effect Style, as shown in Figure 11-10. Hover your mouse cursor over any style for a preview. Note that you can access additional styles by clicking the More Styles arrow in the right of the Ribbon.

 Eliminate all formatting changes applied to your chart by clicking the Reset Graphic button in the far right of the Ribbon.

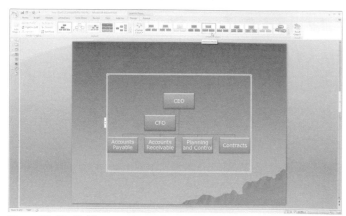

Figure 11-10: Modify an org chart style

Modify an Organization Chart's Color

1. Open a presentation in PowerPoint.

2. To change the colors of your chart, derived from your theme's colors, select the chart and in the Ribbon, click the Design tab and then SmartArt Tools.

3. In the SmartArt Styles group, click Change Colors and choose your desired color from the drop-down palette, as shown in Figure 11-11. Hover your mouse cursor over any color for a preview of the new color.

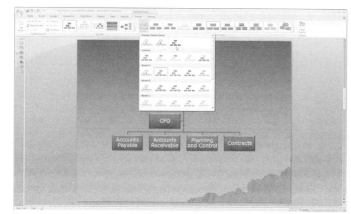

Figure 11-11: Change the color of your org chart

Modify an Organization Chart's Hanging Layout

1. Open a presentation in PowerPoint.

2. Select the shape in the org chart that you want to modify the hanging layout.

3. In the Ribbon, click the Design/SmartArt Tools tab above it.

4. In the Create Graphic group, click Layout and then choose one of the following layout types, all shown in Figures 11-12 and 11-13:

   - **Standard:** Centers all the shapes below the selected shape.

   - **Both:** Centers the selected shape above the shapes below it and arranges those shapes into columns with two shapes in each row.

   - **Left Hanging:** Positions the selected shape to the right and left aligns the shapes below.

   - **Right Hanging:** Positions the selected shape to the left and right aligns the shapes below.

   Note that you can also select a shape and click the Right To Left button in the Create Graphic group in the Ribbon to switch between right and left positions. Finally, you can select a shape and promote (move up a level) or demote (move down a level) it.

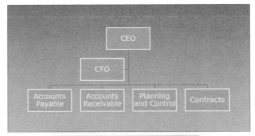

Figure 11-12: Modify an org chart's hanging layout to Standard or Both

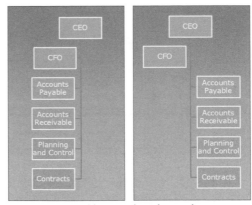

Figure 11-13: Modify an org chart's hanging layout to Left Hanging or Right Hanging

Format Shapes and Text in an Organization Chart

1. Open a presentation in PowerPoint.

2. Select your organization chart. Then select your desired shape.

3. Do any or all of the following:

   • Select and drag your shape to a new location on the chart.

   • Click the Format tab and in the Shapes group, click Change Shape and choose a different shape from the drop-down palette.

   • Click the Format tab and in the Shapes group, click Larger or Smaller to size your shape. You can also place your mouse cursor over a corner and drag to your desired size, as shown in Figure 11-14.

   • Click the Format tab and in the Shapes Styles group, select a different shape outline style. Hover your mouse button over a style to preview it.

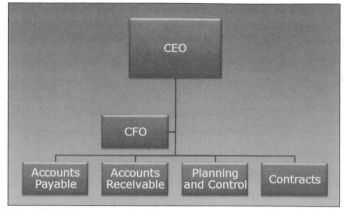

Figure 11-14: Size your org chart shape

- Click the Format tab and in the Shapes Styles group, click Shape Fill and choose a different color for your shape. You can also choose a gradient or even a photo for your shape, as shown in Figure 11-15.

- Click the Format tab and in the Shapes Styles group, click Shape Outline and choose a different color, line weight, or line style (for example, dashed) for your shape.

- Click the Format tab and in the Shapes Styles group, click Shape Effects and choose a different effect, such as a shadow, glow, or bevel for your shape.

- Click the Home tab and in the Font group, change the font size, style, or color of the text in a shape.

- Click the Format tab and in the WordArt group, change the text fill, text outline, and text effects of the text in a shape.

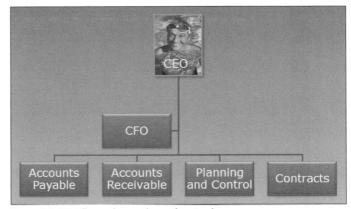

Figure 11-15: Fill your shape with your favorite photo

Import an Organization Chart from Word or Excel

1. Open a presentation in PowerPoint.

2. Navigate to the slide on which you want to put your organization chart.

3. In either Word or Excel, select your organization chart and click Ctrl+C, as shown in Figure 11-16.

4. In PowerPoint, click Ctrl+V. Your chart is inserted on the slide, as shown in Figure 11-17. You can further format the org chart as desired in PowerPoint.

 Note that you can also copy and paste SmartArt Graphics between Word 2007, Excel 2007, and PowerPoint 2007

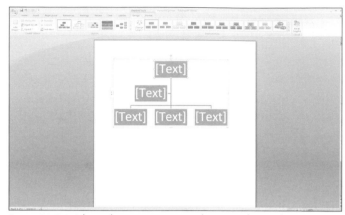

Figure 11-16: Select and copy an organization chart in Word or Excel . . .

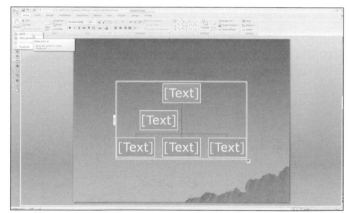

Figure 11-17: . . . and paste it into PowerPoint

Create a Diagram or Flowchart

1. Open a presentation in PowerPoint. Navigate to the slide on which you want to put your diagram or flowchart.

2. In the Ribbon, click the Insert tab. In the Illustrations group, click SmartArt.

3. In the Choose SmartArt Graphic dialog box, choose your desired diagram type from the list on the left. We chose Cycle for our diagram. We chose Process for our flowchart.

4. Next, choose your desired diagram layout, as shown in Figure 11-18. We chose Basic Cycle for our diagram and Basic Bending Process for our flowchart. Click OK. Your diagram or flowchart appears on your slide.

5. To add text to the diagram or flowchart, click in the Text box and type. You can also enter your text in the Text pane. Click the Text pane button in the Ribbon and enter your text in the pane, as shown in Figure 11-19.

     To manually modify the size of the diagram or flowchart, select the diagram and drag the corner sizing handle on the border, which proportionally resizes the object.

     Note that on a flowchart, the red connector dots indicate locked connectors, while green connector dots indicate unlocked connectors. *Locked connectors* move with the shape. To unlock a connector, simply select the connection point and drag it away from the shape.

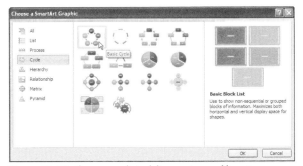

Figure 11-18: Choose your desired diagram type and layout

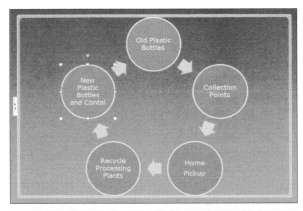

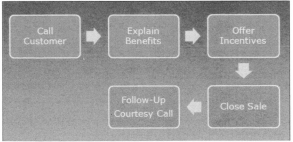

Figure 11-19: Add text to your diagram or flowchart

Add and Delete Shapes in a Diagram or Flowchart

1. Open a presentation in PowerPoint.

2. Select your diagram or flowchart. Then select the existing shape closest to where you would like to add a shape.

3. In the Ribbon, click the Design/SmartArt Tools tab.

4. In the Create Graphic group, click the arrow under Add Shape and choose one of the following from the submenu, as shown in Figure 11-20:

   • **Add Shape After:** Adds a shape after the existing shape.

   • **Add Shape Before:** Adds a shape before the existing shape.

5. To delete a shape, click its border and press Delete.

6. To add text to a shape, simply click in the shape and type.

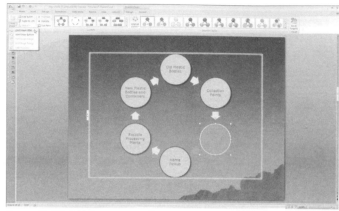

Figure 11-20: Add shapes to your diagram

 Note that when you add a shape in Process type charts, such as flowcharts, you also add a connector.

Convert a Diagram Type

1. Open a presentation in PowerPoint.

2. To convert your diagram to another type, select the diagram and in the Ribbon, click the Design/SmartArt Tools tab.

3. In the Layout Group, click the More button, just to the right of the visible layout thumbnails. Select your desired type and then layout from the Choose A SmartArt Graphic dialog box, as shown in Figure 11-21.

4. We converted our cycle diagram to a pyramid, as shown in Figure 11-22. Note that you can also change process diagrams (flowcharts) to other types as well. After converting to another type, you may have to rearrange the elements in your diagram, as well as modify your text attributes.

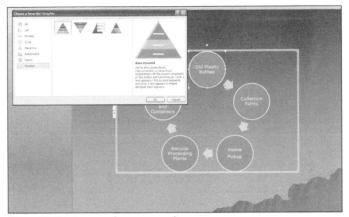

Figure 11-21: Convert a diagram to another type

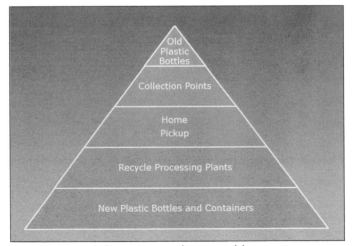

Figure 11-22: A cycle diagram is converted to a pyramid diagram

Convert a Diagram or Flowchart Layout

1. Open a presentation in PowerPoint.

2. To convert your diagram or flowchart to another layout, select it and in the Ribbon, click the Design/SmartArt Tools tab.

3. In the Layout Group, choose your new layout. To access additional layout styles, click the More button, just to the right of the visible layout thumbnails. We converted our Basic Cycle diagram layout to a Text Cycle layout, as shown in Figure 11-23. After converting to another layout, you may have to rearrange the elements in your diagram or flowchart, as well as modify your text attributes.

Figure 11-23: Convert a diagram's layout

Modify a Diagram or Flowchart Style

1. Open a presentation in PowerPoint.

2. To modify the overall style of the diagram or flowchart, select it and in the Ribbon, click the Design/SmartArt Tools tab.

3. From the SmartArt Styles group, choose your desired style, as shown in Figure 11-24.

4. We chose the White Outline style, shown in Figure 11-24.

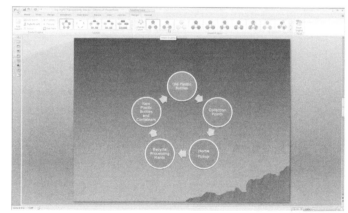

Figure 11-24: Choose from many diagram styles

Modify a Diagram or Flowchart's Color

1. Open a presentation in PowerPoint.

2. To change the colors of your diagram or flowchart, derived from your theme's colors, select it and in the Ribbon, click the Design/SmartArt Tools tab.

3. In the SmartArt Styles group, click Change Colors and choose your desired color from the drop-down palette, as shown in Figure 11-25. Hover your mouse cursor over any color for a preview of the new color.

Format Shapes and Text in a Diagram or Flowchart

1. Open a presentation in PowerPoint.

2. Select your diagram. Then select your desired shape.

3. Do any or all of the following:

   • Select and drag your shape to a new location on the diagram.

   • Click the Format tab and in the Shapes group, click Change Shape and choose a different shape from the drop down palette, shown in Figure 11-26.

   • Click the Format tab and in the Shapes group, click Larger or Smaller to size your shape. You can also place your mouse cursor over a corner and drag to your desired size.

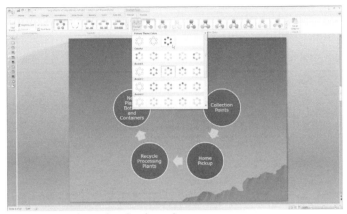

Figure 11-25: Change the color of your diagram

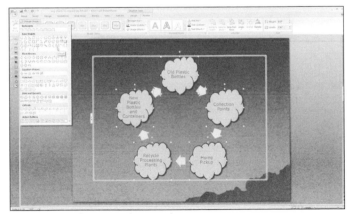

Figure 11-26: Change your diagram's shape

- Click the Format tab and in the Shapes Styles group, select a different shape outline style. Hover your mouse button over a style to preview it.

- Click the Format tab and in the Shapes Styles group, click Shape Fill and choose a different color for your shape. You can also choose a gradient or even a photo for your shape.

- Click the Format tab and in the Shapes Styles group, click Shape Outline and choose a different color, line weight, or line style (for example, dashed) for your shape.

- Click the Format tab and in the Shapes Styles group, click Shape Effects and choose a different effect, such as a shadow, glow, or bevel for your shape.

- Click the Home tab and in the Font group, change the font size, style, or color of the text in a shape.

- Click the Format tab and in the WordArt group, change the text fill, text outline, and text effects of the text in a shape.

- Click the Design tab and in the Create Graphic group, click Add Bullet to add a text bullet after your existing text.

We jazzed up our diagram via the various formatting options, as shown in Figure 11-27.

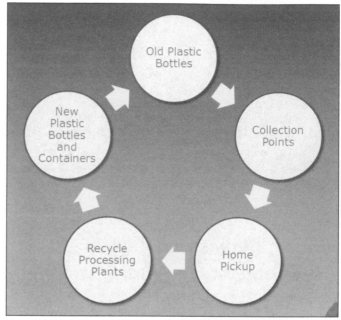

Figure 11-27: Format your diagram with colors, fills, and effects

Part III
Adding a Dash of Pizzazz with Multimedia

The 5th Wave   By Rich Tennant

"Okay-looks like the 'Dissolve' transition in my presentation needs adjusting."

Integrating Sound and Movies

*I*f photos and illustrations add icing to your presentations, then sound and movies are the proverbial cherry on top. You can really grab the attention of your audience by adding audio and video elements to your presentation. What's great is that it's easy to do. A couple of menu commands are all it takes to integrate sound and movies into your slide show.

If you're short on content, PowerPoint offers quite a few media clips in its library. Music can also be imported from your own CDs or from MP3 files you have created or purchased online. Many stock photo Web sites also offer reasonably priced audio and video clips. In addition to video, you can add animated GIFs to your presentations. Animated GIFs have small file sizes and can be very effective in demonstrating a sequence.

This chapter gives you the scoop on how to integrate sound and movies into your presentations and really bring them to life.

Get ready to . . .

Insert Sound from a File

1. Open a presentation in PowerPoint.

2. In Normal view, in the Slides pane, select the slide to which you want to add sound.

3. In the Ribbon, click the Insert tab, as shown in Figure 12-1.

4. In the Media Clips group, click the arrow under Sound and select Sound From File from the drop-down list.

5. Navigate to and select the sound file you want and then click OK. A sound icon appears on your slide, as shown in Figure 12-2.

6. In the alert box that appears, indicate whether you want the sound to play automatically when you display the slide or whether you want the sound to play when you click the sound icon.

7. To test the sound quality, double-click the sound icon on your slide. If you are in a Slide Show view, a single click will do it.

 PowerPoint accepts the following sound file formats: WAV, WV, MP3, MPEG-4, Audio, AIF, AIFF, AIFC, MIDI, MID, KAR, MOV, MOOV, SFIL, RSRC, ALAW, AU, SND, and ULAW.

 Only a .wav (Waveform Audio Format) can be embedded in your presentation. Note that by default, all .wav files larger than 100 KB are linked rather than embedded. You can increase the size of an embedded file up to a max of 50 MB, but you may suffer a performance slowdown. (See the section "Edit Movie and Sound Options," later in this chapter, for details.) All other formats are linked to your presentation, so be sure to include the links with your presentation by saving it as a PowerPoint Package.

 You can also play a sound across multiple slides. (See the upcoming section "Edit Movie and Sound Options" for details.)

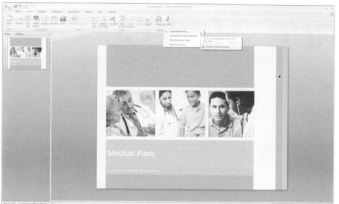

Figure 12-1: Insert a sound from a file onto your slide

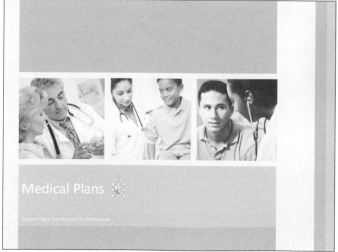

Figure 12-2: Sound is indicated by an icon

Insert Sound from the Clip Organizer

1. Open a presentation in PowerPoint.

2. In Normal view, in the Slides pane, select the slide in which you want to add sound.

3. In the Ribbon, click the Insert tab.

4. In the Media Clips group, click the arrow under Sound and select Sound From Clip Organizer from the drop-down list.

5. In the alert box that appears, indicate whether you want to include thousands of additional clip art images and photos from Microsoft Office Online.

6. Choose your desired sound from the Clip Art task pane, shown in Figure 12-3. An alert box asks whether you want the sound to play automatically when you display the slide, as shown in Figure 12-4.

7. Click Automatically or When Clicked. If you click When Clicked, the sound will play when you click the sound icon. (Note that if you choose to hide the sound icon, you must elect to play the sound automatically.) A sound icon appears on your slide.

8. To test the sound quality, double-click the sound icon on your slide. To remove the sound, simply select and delete the icon.

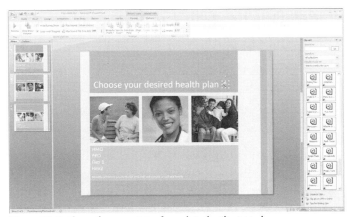

Figure 12-3: Choose from a variety of sounds in the Clip Art task pane

Figure 12-4: Choose whether to play the sound automatically or manually

Insert Sound from a CD

1. Open a presentation in PowerPoint.

2. In Normal view, in the Slides pane, select the slide you want to add sound to.

3. Make sure that your CD is in your CD drive.

4. In the Ribbon, click the Insert tab.

5. In the Media Clips group, click the arrow under Sound and select Play CD Audio Track from the drop-down list.

6. In the Insert CD Audio dialog box, select your desired track (song) or tracks, as shown in Figure 12-5.

7. Set your Timing, Play, and Display options:

   • Check Loop Until Stopped to have your music play repeatedly until you stop it.

   • Click the Sound Volume icon to access the volume slider.

   • Choose whether to hide the sound icon during your slide show.

8. Click OK.

9. A dialog box asks whether you want the sound to play automatically when you display the slide or when you click the CD icon; click your choice. A CD icon appears on your slide, as shown in Figure 12-6.

10. To test the sound quality, double-click the CD icon on your slide.

 Remember, the music from the CD is not embedded into your presentation. You must have the actual CD in your CD drive to play the music during your show.

Figure 12-5: Insert an audio track from a CD

Figure 12-6: A CD icon indicates audio from a CD

Record a Sound

1. Open a presentation in PowerPoint.

2. In Normal view, in the Slides pane, select the slide to which you want to add your sound. (Sounds, also referred to as *comments* in this case, are meant to be recorded on a single slide. To record a voice throughout the presentation, see the next section, "Record a Narration.")

3. In the Ribbon, click the Insert tab.

4. In the Media Clips group, click the arrow next to Sound and choose Record Sound from the drop-down list, as shown in Figure 12-7.

 In order to record a comment or a narration, make sure that your computer is outfitted with a sound card, a microphone, and speakers.

5. In the Record Sound dialog box, name your sound, as shown in Figure 12-8.

6. In the Record Sound dialog box, click the Record button (the red circle) and speak into the microphone.

7. When you're finished recording your sound, click the Stop button (the blue square).

8. To play the sound back, click the Play button (the blue triangle).

9. Repeat Steps 2 through 7 for any other slides you want to add sound to.

10. Click OK. A sound icon appears on the slide.

 If the quality of the sound is vital, you may want to look into free recording programs, such as Audacity, which provide more controls and produce a superior-quality sound over the Windows recorder.

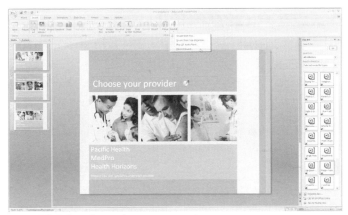

Figure 12-7: Record a sound in your presentation

Figure 12-8: Name your sound and record using controls

Record a Narration

1. Open a presentation in PowerPoint. (*Narrations* are designed to run through an entire presentation. You may want to use them for Web or self-running presentations. For short voice recordings on a single slide, see "Record a Sound.")

2. In Normal view, in the Slide pane, select the slide you want to start your narration on.

3. In the Ribbon, click the Slide Show tab.

4. In the Set Up group, click Record Narration.

5. In the Record Narration dialog box, shown in Figure 12-9, perform the following actions:

   • Click the Set Microphone Level button to specify your desired volume. Click OK.

   • Adjust the quality by clicking the Change Quality button. In the Sound Selection dialog box, shown in Figure 12-10, choose from CD Quality (highest) to Telephone Quality (lowest) from the Name drop-down list and then click OK. Note that the higher the sound quality, the larger the file size.

6. Choose whether or not to link your narration to your presentation. If you choose to link your narration, click the Browse button and select the folder in which you want to save your narration file. If you don't link your narration, it will be embedded into your presentation. Linking larger narrations enables your presentation file to remain at a manageable size. Remember to include the linked narration file with your presentation file on your hard drive or on any external media.

7. Click OK.

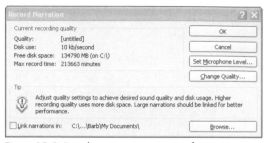

Figure 12-9: Record a voiceover, or narration, for your presentation

Figure 12-10: Specify the sound quality of your narration

Note that PowerPoint can play only one sound file at a time. Therefore, if you have other sounds that play automatically in your presentation, the narration overrides those sounds.

8. If you chose the first slide in your presentation in Step 2, proceed to Step 9. If you selected another slide in your presentation in Step 2, a second, smaller Record Narration alert box appears. Click either Current Slide or First Slide to indicate where you want your narration to begin.

9. Your presentation now appears in Slide Show view. Speak your narration into the microphone. When you're done with the narration for that slide, click the slide to advance to the next slide. Continue your narration for the next slide. Repeat these steps for your entire presentation.

 You can pause your narration by right-clicking the slide and choosing Pause Narration from the context menu. To resume your narration, choose Resume Narration using the same method.

 If you make a mistake, you can rerecord part of the narration. Go to the slide you want to rerecord and follow Steps 1 through 7. When you're done rerecording the portions you want to change, press Esc and go to Step 11.

10. When the black "end of presentation" screen appears, click it. Your narration is saved.

11. A message appears, asking you whether you'd also like to save the slide timings (shown below each slide). If you click Save, your presentation will appear in Slide Sorter view with timings displayed under each slide, as shown in Figure 12-11. If you click Don't Save, you will return to your first slide. To preview a narration, double-click the Sound icon.

 You can run your slide show with the narration but without your saved timings. Click the Slide Show tab and in the Set Up group, click Set Up Slide Show and under Advance Slides, click Manually, as shown in Figure 12-12.

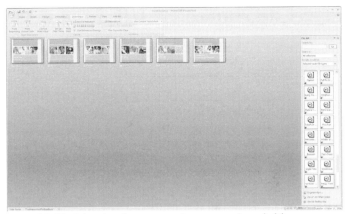

Figure 12-11: Slide timings for your narration appear under each slide

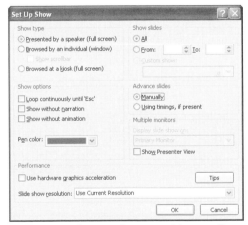

Figure 12-12: Choose to advance your slides manually

Insert an Animated GIF from a File

1. Open a presentation in PowerPoint.

2. In Normal view, in the Slides pane, select the slide to which you want to add your animated GIF.

3. Click the Insert tab.

4. In the Media Clips group, click the arrow under Movie and choose Movie From File.

5. Navigate to and select your animated GIF file and click OK.

6. The first frame of the animated GIF appears on your slide, as shown in Figure 12-13.

7. To preview the animated GIF, click the Animations tab in the Ribbon and then click the Preview button at the far left.

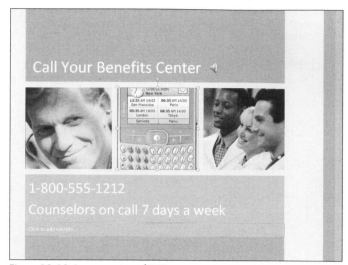

Figure 12-13: Insert an animated GIF into your presentation

Insert a Movie from a File

1. Open a presentation in PowerPoint.

2. In Normal view, in the Slides pane, select the slide to which you want to add a movie.

3. Click the Insert tab.

4. In the Media Clips group, click the arrow under Movie and choose Movie from File, as shown in Figure 12-14.

5. Navigate to and select your movie file and click Insert. The first frame of the movie appears on your slide..

6. In the dialog box that asks whether you want the movie to play automatically when you display the slide, click Automatically or When Clicked. If you click When Clicked, the movie will play when you click the movie frame.

7. To preview the movie, double-click the frame on your slide.

 PowerPoint accepts the following movie file formats: AVI, DVR-MS, MP2V, MP3, M3U, MPA, M1V, MPE, MPEG, MPG, .ASF, WP2, WPL. WM, WMD, WMV, WMX.

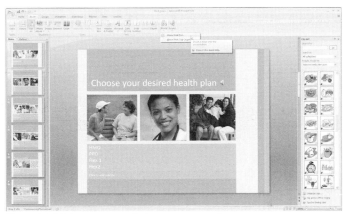

Figure 12-14: Insert a movie clip into your presentation

Insert an Animated GIF or Movie from the Clip Organizer

1. Open a presentation in PowerPoint.

2. In Normal view, in the Slides pane, select the slide to which you want to add a movie.

3. Click the Insert tab.

4. In the Media Clips group, click the arrow under Movie and choose Movie From Clip Organizer.

5. The Clip Art task pane appears, as shown in Figure 12-15. If you know where your GIF or movie clip is located, scroll through the library and select it. If you're unsure, you can enter the name or keyword of your desired file in the Search For field. You can restrict your search to just Movies or Animated GIFs by checking your desired media types and file formats in the Selected Media File Types drop-down list. Click Go. Locate and then click your desired file in the library.

6. If you insert a movie, a dialog box asks whether you want the movie to play automatically when you display the slide. Click Yes or No. If you click No, the movie will play when you click the movie frame. If you insert a GIF, you don't see a dialog box. The first frame of the GIF or movie appears on your slide, as shown in Figure 12-16.

7. To preview the movie, double-click the frame on your slide. To preview the animated GIF, click the Animations tab in the Ribbon and then click the Preview button at the far left.

 You can preview any clip by positioning your mouse cursor over the thumbnail in the Clip Art task pane library and clicking the down arrow. Select Preview/Properties from the drop-down list. Click the arrow in the Preview/Properties dialog box to play the clip.

Figure 12-15: Insert a movie clip from the Clip Organizer

Figure 12-16: The first frame of your movie appears on the slide

Resize a Movie

1. Open a presentation in PowerPoint.

2. In Normal view, in the Slides pane, select the slide that contains your movie clip.

3. Select the clip on the slide.

4. On the Options tab, under Movie Tools, in the Size group, click the Dialog Box Launcher in the bottom right corner.

5. Click the Size tab and enter your desired Height and Width dimensions or percentages, as shown in Figure 12-17. You can also just position your mouse cursor over one of the corner sizing handles. Drag the movie frame larger or smaller, as shown in Figure 12-18. Press the Ctrl key to keep the center of the movie in the same location. Press the Shift key to constrain the proportions while sizing.

6. Click OK.

 To prevent a movie from skipping, it is advisable to check Best Scale from Slide Show in the Size tab in Step 5.

Edit Movie and Sound Options

1. Open a presentation in PowerPoint.

2. In Normal view, select the slide that contains your sound or movie clip.

3. Select the clip on the slide.

4. In the Ribbon, click the Options tab.

Figure 12-17: Launch your Size dialog box

Figure 12-18: Resize your movie manually

5. Select either Movie Tools or Sound Tools.

6. Specify your settings in the Movie Options or Sound Options group (see Figure 12-19):

- **Play Movie:** Choose from When Clicked, Automatically, or Play Across Slides. When you choose the latter, the movie continues to play when you advance to the next slide. If you choose this option, you must then click the Animations tab and then Custom Animation in the Animations group. In the Custom Animations task pane, click the movie play effect (line with triangle) and then click the down arrow and select Effect Options from the drop-down list. Under Stop playing, click After and specify the number of slides (see Figure 12-20).

- **Loop Until Stopped:** The movie or sound plays repeatedly until you stop it.

- **Rewind Movie After Playing:** The movie automatically rewinds to the first frame after playing once.

- **Slide Sound volume:** Click the icon to access the volume slider.

- **Hide During Show:** Icons and frames are hidden during the slide show.

- **Play Full Screen:** The movie plays full screen. When it's completed, the slide returns on-screen.

- **Max Sound File Size:** By default. .wav sound files are linked, rather than embedded, if they're bigger than 100KB. You can increase that threshold. Beware that embedding too large a file may impact PowerPoint's performance.

7. Click OK.

 You can use the Custom Animation task pane to play, pause, and stop a movie. You can also use this task pane to further animate a sound or movie object. For example, you can have the first frame of your movie or your sound icon move into the frame and begin playing. See Chapter 11 for further details on animation.

Figure 12-19: Edit your movie and sound options

Figure 12-20: Choose to play a movie over multiple slides

Incorporate Hyperlinks and Transitions

You may think a basic office program such as PowerPoint is incapable of adding any snap, crackle, and pop to your presentations. Think again. Underneath PowerPoint's conservative attire lies a whole bevy of special effects that you can apply to your slides. If you need to jump to a Web site or to another file or presentation during your slide show, you simply insert a hyperlink. Advancing from one slide to the next can be elegant and unobtrusive with slow fades, or dynamic and active with wipes and spins. With this chapter's help, your presentations will be snapping, crackling, and popping to their heart's content!

Chapter

13

Get ready to . . .

Create a Hyperlink within a Presentation

1. Open a presentation in PowerPoint.

2. In Normal view, go to the slide that contains the element you want to use as your source link in the hyperlink.

3. Choose the element (we chose a small circular shape) and then in the Ribbon, click the Animations tab.

4. In the Links group, click Hyperlink, as shown in Figure 13-1.

5. In the Insert Hyperlink dialog box, click the Place In This Document option under Link To, as shown in Figure 13-2.

6. Select your desired destination link under Select A Place In This Document. Select from the slides or a custom show within your presentation. If you select a custom show, you can select the Show And Return option, which will take the display back to the source link after the show has played. For more on custom shows, see Chapter 16.

7. Click OK.

8. To test your hyperlink, run your presentation by clicking the Slide Show tab in the Ribbon and then clicking From Current Slide. You can also click the Slide Show button in the bottom right of the window. Note that when you hover your cursor over the hyperlink, the arrow becomes a pointing hand, indicating a link.

 Hyperlinks are links from one slide to another slide, a custom show (a subpresentation within your main presentation), a Web site, an e-mail address, or a file. The hyperlink can be text, a picture, an AutoShape, a chart, WordArt, or an action button. (We describe action buttons later in this chapter.)

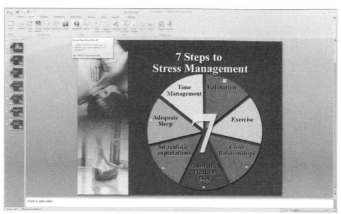

Figure 13-1: Assign a hyperlink to text or objects

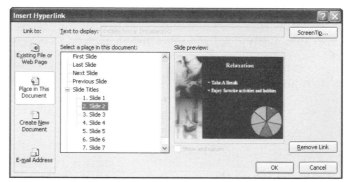

Figure 13-2: Choose a destination link
Photo Credit: Corbis Images, PhotoDisc/Getty Image

Insert a Hyperlink to an Existing File or Web Site

1. Open a presentation in PowerPoint.

2. In Normal view, go to the slide that contains the element you want to use as your source link in the hyperlink.

3. Choose the element (we chose a small circular shape) and then in the Ribbon, click the Animations tab.

4. In the Links group, click Hyperlink.

5. In the Insert Hyperlink dialog box, click Existing File Or Web Page under Link To, as shown in Figure 13-3. You can also click Recent Files or Browsed Pages to locate files or pages recently accessed or browsed. Finally, you can click the Browse The Web icon (a globe and magnifying glass) to launch your Web browser to locate and select your desired Web site.

6. Navigate to your desired file or type your Web site URL in the Address field.

7. Click OK.

 Note that a hyperlink is automatically created when you type a Web site URL on a slide in your presentation outline. Note that the link is active in Slide Show view only. Hyperlinks are indicated by a pointing finger icon, as shown in Figure 13-4

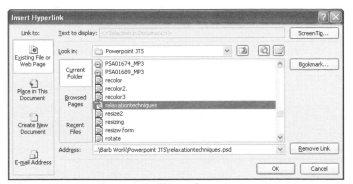

Figure 13-3: Create a hyperlink to a file or Web site

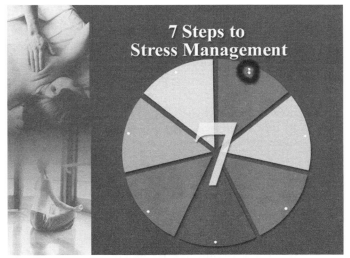

Figure 13-4: Hyperlinks are indicated by a pointing finger icon

Insert a Hyperlink to a New File

1. Open a presentation in PowerPoint.

2. In Normal view, go to the slide that contains the element you want to use as your source link in the hyperlink.

3. Choose the element (we chose a small circular AutoShape) and then in the Ribbon, click the Animations tab.

4. In the Links group, click Hyperlink.

5. In the Insert Hyperlink dialog box, click Create New Document under Link To.

6. Type the name of your new document, as shown in Figure 13-5.

7. Click the Change button to navigate to the location where you would like to save the new document. Note that the path to that location will be recorded.

8. In the Create New Document dialog box, shown in Figure 13-6, select the type of file format you want for your new document. For our document, we selected a .docx file format.

9. Choose whether to edit the new document now or later. If you choose now, the program to create your new document launches. You can then enter any text you want to appear when the document is opened. If you choose later, the program launches, and a new document is created when the user first clicks the hyperlink during the slide show. The program that is launched depends on the file format you chose in Step 8. When we click our hyperlink, Word launches because our file format is a .docx file.

10. Click OK.

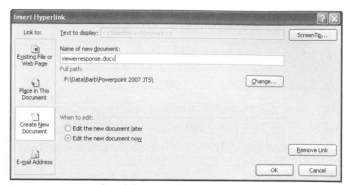

Figure 13-5: Create a hyperlink to a new file

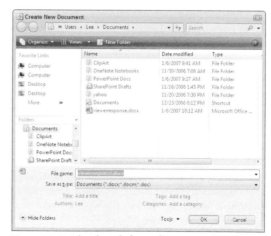

Figure 13-6: Select the right format for your new document

Insert a Hyperlink to an E-Mail Address

1. Open a presentation in PowerPoint.

2. In Normal view, go to the slide that contains the element you want to use as your source link in the hyperlink.

3. Choose the element (we chose a small circular AutoShape) and then in the Ribbon, click the Animations tab.

4. In the Links group, click Hyperlink.

5. In the Insert Hyperlink dialog box, select E-Mail Address under Link To, as shown in Figure 13-7.

6. Type your desired e-mail address. (You can also select an e-mail address from the Recently Used E-Mail Addresses box.)

7. Type the subject you want to appear in the e-mail subject line.

8. Click OK.

9. When the hyperlink is clicked in the slide show, the default e-mail client launches, and a new message window opens, as shown in Figure 13-8.

 Note that a hyperlink is automatically created when you type an e-mail address on a slide in your presentation outline. Note that the link is active in Slide Show view only.

Figure 13-7: Create a hyperlink to an e-mail address

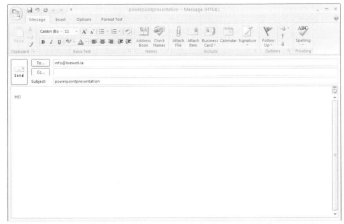

Figure 13-8: The default e-mail client is launched when you click the hyperlink

Insert a Hyperlink to Another Presentation

1. Open a presentation in PowerPoint.

2. In Normal view, go to the slide that contains the element you want to use as your source link in the hyperlink.

3. Choose the element (we chose a small circular AutoShape) and then in the Ribbon, click the Animations tab.

4. In the Links group, click Hyperlink.

5. In the Insert Hyperlink dialog box, click Existing File Or Web Page under Link To, as shown in Figure 13-9.

6. Navigate to and select the presentation that contains the slide you want to designate as your destination link.

7. Click the Bookmark button in the top right corner. In the Select Place In Document dialog box, shown in Figure 13-10, select the slide you want to link to.

8. Click OK and OK again to exit the dialog box and apply the hyperlink.

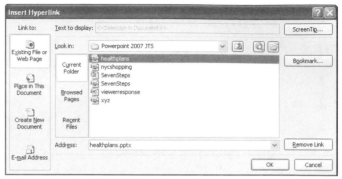

Figure 13-9: Create a hyperlink to another presentation

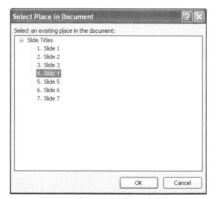

Figure 13-10: Choose your desired slide within the presentation

Change the Color of Hyperlinked Text

1. Open a presentation in PowerPoint.

2. In the Ribbon, click the Design tab.

3. Click Colors and scroll down to Create New Theme Colors.

4. In the Create New Theme Colors dialog box (see Figure 13-11), select a new color from the Hyperlink or Followed Hyperlink drop-down lists.

5. Select a color from either the Theme or Standard color palettes. You can also select More Colors to select from a Custom color palette. Click OK. (For more on Standard and Custom colors, see Chapter 8.)

6. Click Apply. The colors of your hyperlinked text before you click them and after they have been clicked change, as shown in Figure 13-12.

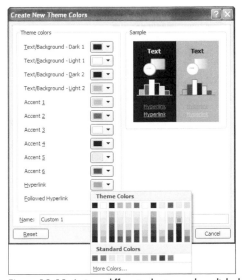

Figure 13-11: Assign a different color to your hyperlinked text

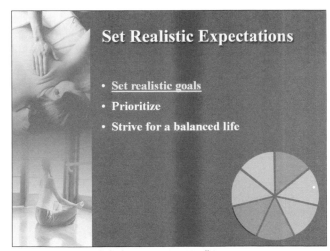

Figure 13-12: Hyperlinked text now appears yellow
Photo Credit: Corbis Images, PhotoDisc/Getty Images

Show Highlights or Play Sounds on Hyperlinks

1. Open a presentation in PowerPoint.

2. Select the hyperlinked text or object.

3. Click the Insert tab. In the Links Group, click Action.

4. In the Action Settings dialog box, shown in Figure 13-13, select one of the following:

   • **Mouse Click:** This option applies the action when the mouse is clicked on the hyperlink object.

   • **Mouse Over:** This applies the action when the mouse is pointed to the hyperlink object.

5. Assign the action to the hyperlink:

   • **Hyperlink To:** If you already have a destination link established, you can ignore this setting. If you select a custom show, type the name of the show. If you select a URL, type the location of the Web site. If you select another PowerPoint presentation or file, navigate to the location on your hard drive and select the file.

   • **Play Sound:** Select this check box to have your hyperlink object play a sound when you click or point to it. Select your desired sound from the drop-down list. Select a PowerPoint preset sound or your own sound file. Note that the sound must be in the .wav file format.

   • **Highlight Click:** Select this check box to have your hyperlink object highlighted when you click or point to it, as shown in Figure 13-14.

6. Click OK.

Figure 13-13: Assign sounds or highlighting to your hyperlink object

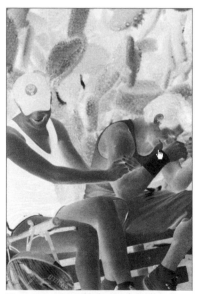

Figure 13-14: Highlight your hyperlink object by clicking or pointing with your mouse
Photo Credit: PhotoSpin

Insert an Action Button

1. Open a presentation in PowerPoint.

2. Go to the slide on which you want to insert an Action button.

3. Click the Insert tab. In the Illustration group, click Shapes and choose your desired Action button from the drop-down palette.

4. Click on the slide to place the button.

5. In the Action Settings dialog box, shown in Figure 13-15, specify your desired action. Select Mouse Click or Mouse Over by clicking the desired tab. Then set the destination link for your hyperlink. You can also assign a sound to the action. For details on these settings, see the preceding section, "Show Highlights or Play Sounds on Hyperlinks."

6. Click OK.

7. On our slide, shown in Figure 13-16, we chose Previous and Next buttons. When the user clicks, he goes to the previous or next slide. We also resized our buttons by simply dragging a corner sizing handle.

 Insert action buttons (such as Previous, Next, and Play) to help your viewers navigate through your presentation, and they're especially helpful for self-running presentations on the Web or in kiosks.

 You can also insert action buttons on all your slides. Simply insert the action buttons on your slide master(s). For more on slide masters, see Chapter 4.

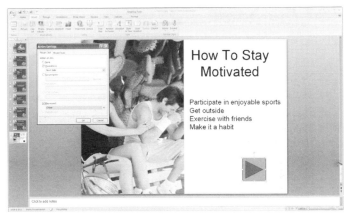

Figure 13-15: Choose your button style

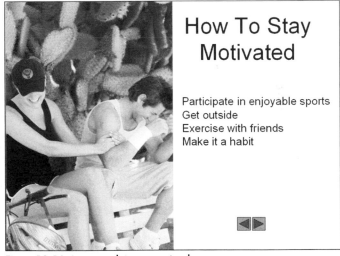

Figure 13-16: Arrange and size your actions buttons
Photo Credit: PhotoSpin

Add the Same Transition to All Slides

1. Open a presentation in PowerPoint.

2. In Normal View, click the Home tab.

3. In the Slides pane, select a slide thumbnail.

4. In the Ribbon, click the Animations tab.

5. In the Transition To This Slide group, select your desired transition, as shown in Figure 13-17. To access additional transitions, click the bottom arrow to the right of the transition effects.

6. Click Apply To All.

7. Specify the speed of your transitions. Select Slow, Medium, or Fast.

8. You can also attach a sound to your transition. Click on the down arrow to select one of the presets from the PowerPoint library or select Other Sound from the drop-down list to navigate to your own sound file.

9. Choose whether to automatically advance to the next slide after a specified number of seconds or to advance by clicking your mouse.

10. To preview the transition, shown in Figure 13-18, hover your mouse over the transition effect. To play the slide show from your current slide forward, click Slide Show at the bottom right of the window.

 To remove a slide transition, select a slide thumbnail and click the Animations tab. In the Transition To This Slide group, click No Transition.

 To remove all of the slide transitions, select a slide thumbnail and click the Animations tab. In the Transition To This Slide group, click No Transition and then Apply To All.

Figure 13-17: Apply transitions to your slides

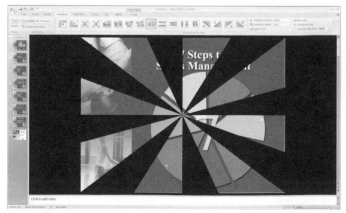

Figure 13-18: Preview your transition effect

Add a Different Transition to Each Slide

1. Open a presentation in PowerPoint.

2. In Normal view, click the Home tab.

3. In the Slides pane, select a slide thumbnail.

4. In the Ribbon, click the Animations tab.

5. In the Transition To This Slide group, select your desired transition, as shown in Figure 13-19. To access additional transitions, click the arrow to the right of the transition effects).

6. Repeat Steps 2 through 4 for all the slides in your presentation. To change a transition, simply select your desired slide and choose a different transition. To preview the transition, as shown in Figure 13-20, hover your mouse over the transition effect.

7. For specifying transition settings, see the earlier section, "Add the Same Transition to All Slides."

 Transitions are effects used to advance from one slide to the next. Although transitions are fun, be careful about using too many different kinds of transitions. You want your audience to pay attention to your content, not be distracted by your special effects, or worse, get motion sickness.

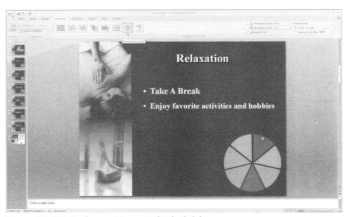

Figure 13-19: Apply transitions to individual slides

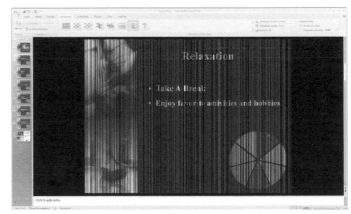

Figure 13-20: Preview the transition effect

Incorporate Animation

*I*f the previous chapter on hyperlinks and transitions doesn't add enough pizzazz to your presentations, you may want to step it up a bit and employ custom animations to the elements on your slides. You can easily have your text fly in from the left and then hide or change color after it has played. Or you can create a custom motion path and have your object follow a map on your slide. If motion isn't enough, you can easily attach sounds, such as camera clicks or voltage zaps, to your animations.

This chapter shows you how to employ animation for added emphasis and impact in your presentations.

Get ready to . . .

Apply Standard Animation Effects

1. Open a presentation in PowerPoint.

2. In Normal view, under the Slides tab, select your desired slide(s) for the animation.

3. In the Ribbon, click the Animations tab.

4. On the slide, select the text or object you want to animate.

5. In the Ribbon, in the Animation Group, select your desired standard effect (Fade, Wipe, or Fly-In) from the Animate list. We chose Fade, as shown in Figure 14-1. After the effect is applied, a nonprinting number appears next to your text or object indicating the order of the effect. The number also doesn't appear in the slide show.

6. Click the Preview button, in the far left of the Ribbon, to preview the effect on your displayed slide.

7. Click the Slide Show button, in the bottom right of the window, to play the presentation from your displayed slide forward.

8. To delete the animation effect, select No Animation from the Animate list.

Figure 14-1: Animate your slides
Photo Credit: PhotoSpin

Create a Motion Path for Animations

1. Open a presentation in PowerPoint.

2. In Normal view, under the Slides tab, select the slide that contains the object for which you want to create a motion path.

3. Select the object on the slide.

4. In the Ribbon, click the Animations tab. In the Animations Group, click Custom Animation.

5. In the Custom Animation task pane, click Add Effect and then select Motion Paths, as shown in Figure 14-2.

6. Choose from the following:

   - **Standard Motion Path:** Choose from one of the standard paths.

   - **Draw Custom Path:** Choose from one of four ways to draw your path. *Freeform* enables you to draw a path with curved (drag) and straight (click and move mouse) lines. *Scribble* enables you to drag curved lines as if you were using a pen on paper, as shown in Figure 14-3. *Line* lets you drag straight lines. And *Curve* lets you draw by clicking where you want your curves.

   - **More Motion Paths:** Choose from additional standard paths.

7. Your motion path appears on the slide. Adjust your path by selecting it and dragging any one of the nodes.

8. Click Play, at the bottom of the pane, to preview the effect on your displayed slide.

9. Click Slide Show, at the bottom of the pane, to play the presentation from your displayed slide forward.

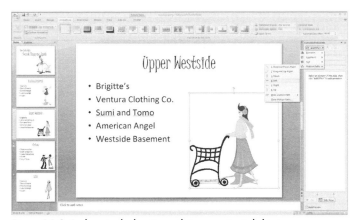

Figure 14-2: Apply a standard motion path to your animated object
Photo Credit: PhotoSpin

Figure 14-3: Draw a custom motion path
Photo Credit: PhotoSpin

Apply a Custom Animation Effect to Text or Objects

1. Open a presentation in PowerPoint.

2. In Normal view, under the Slides tab, select the slide that contains the text or object you want to animate.

3. Select the text or object on the slide. If you select the text box placeholder, all the text within the box will animate. Highlight individual sections of text within the box to have them animate individually.

4. In the Ribbon, click the Animations tab. In the Animations Group, click Custom Animation.

5. In the Custom Animation task pane, shown in Figure 14-4, select how you would like your text or object to appear on the slide by clicking Add Effect and selecting from the following:

   • **Entrance:** The object or text enters the slide show with the animated effect.

   • **Emphasis:** The object or text is animated while it is on the slide.

   • **Exit:** The object or text leaves the slide show with the animated effect.

   • **Motion Paths:** The object or text moves by following a specific path and direction. For details, see the preceding section, "Create a Motion Path for Animations."

6. Choose your desired animation effect from the submenu. Choose More Effects to view the full list of effects. Once applied, the effect is added to the list. A nonprinting number appears next to your text or object, indicating the order of the effect. The number also doesn't appear in the slide show. To rearrange the order, click the Re-Order arrows at the bottom of the pane.

Figure 14-4: Add animation to individual objects and text
Photo Credit: PhotoSpin

Figure 14-5: Specify the direction and speed of your animation effect
Photo Credit: PhotoSpin

7. Specify your animation settings in the Custom Animation pane. Choose how you want your animation to start. Also specify the direction and speed of the animation movement, as shown in Figure 14-5.

8. Click Play, at the bottom of the pane, to preview the effect on your displayed slide, as shown in Figures 14-6 and 14-7. Note the timeline that appears when you play your effects to demonstrate your timing.

9. Click Slide Show, at the bottom of the pane, to play the presentation from your displayed slide forward.

10. To edit an animation, select the effect from the list and click Change. Then follow Steps 5 through 7 in this list.

11. To delete an animation effect, select it and click Remove.

 You can apply animations not only to text and objects, but even diagrams and charts. And remember, objects can consist of AutoShapes, clip art, photos, sounds, and movies.

 You can also animate individual elements of a chart by selecting them in your chart and applying an effect. Then click the down arrow to the right of the effect and, from the context menu, choose Effect Options. Click the Chart Animation or Diagram Animation tab. From the Group chart or Group diagram drop-down list, select an option, such as By Series or By Category. The options you see depend on the type of chart or diagram.

Figure 14-6: The graphic is still . . .
Photo Credit: PhotoSpin

Figure 14-7: . . . and then swivels
Photo Credit: PhotoSpin

Apply Animation to Bullets

1. Open a presentation in PowerPoint.

2. In Normal view, under the Slides tab, select the slide that contains the bulleted text you want to animate.

3. In the Ribbon, click the Animations tab. In the Animations Group, click Custom Animation.

4. Select the first bulleted text.

5. In the Custom Animation task pane, shown in Figure 14-8, choose how you'd like your bulleted text to appear on the slide by clicking Add Effect and then choosing Entrance.

6. From the Entrance submenu, choose your desired animation effect.

7. Leave your Start option set to On Click.

8. Specify your desired speed for the bullet.

9. Click Play, at the bottom of the pane, to preview the effect on your displayed slide.

10. Click Slide Show, at the bottom of the pane, to play the presentation from your displayed slide forward.

Figure 14-8: Animate your bulleted text for more emphasis
Photo Credit: PhotoSpin

Apply Effects Options to Animated Bullets

1. Open a presentation in PowerPoint.

2. In Normal view, under the Slides tab, select the slide that contains the animation effect you want to enhance.

3. In the Ribbon, click the Animations tab. In the Animations Group, click Custom Animation.

4. In the Custom Animation task pane, select your animated effect from the list and then click the down-pointing arrow to the right. You can also select all the effects and click the arrow for the last one in the list.

 To select all your bullets in one fell swoop, click the first bullet and then Shift+click the last bullet. To select multiple nonconsecutive bullets, click the first bullet and then Ctrl+click each of the other bullets.

5. From the menu, choose Effect Options, as shown in Figure 14-9.

6. In the dialog box for your specific animation effect (ours happens to be Faded Swivel), under the Effect tab, select the desired enhancements. For the Faded Swivel effect, your choices are as follows:

- **Sound:** Select a sound effect to attach to your animation. If you select Other Sound, navigate to your desired sound on your hard drive. Set the volume for your sound by clicking the speaker icon.

- **After animation:** Choose whether to dim or hide your text after the animation or after your next mouse click, as shown in Figure 14-10. You can also have your text or object change colors after the animation. We chose gray to have our text turn to gray after animation.

- **Animate text:** Choose whether to have your bulleted text animate all at once or by each word or letter. If you choose by word or letter, specify the percentage of delay between words or letters.

7. Click OK.

8. Click Play to preview the effect on your displayed slide.

9. Click Slide Show to play the presentation from your displayed slide forward.

Figure 14-9: Enhance the effects of your bullets
Photo Credit: PhotoSpin

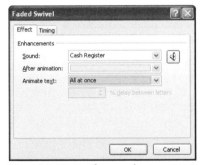

Figure 14-10: Specify your enhancement settings
Photo Credit: PhotoSpin

Apply Effects Options to Animated Text or Objects

1. Open a presentation in PowerPoint.

2. In Normal view, under the Slides tab, select the slide that contains the animation effect you want to enhance.

3. In the Ribbon, click the Animations tab. In the Animations Group, click Custom Animation.

4. In the Custom Animation task pane, select your animated effect from the list.

5. Click the down arrow to the right and then choose Effect Options from the context menu.

6. In the dialog box for your specific animation effect (ours is a Line Custom Motion Path), under the Effect tab, select the desired enhancements. For a motion path, your choices are as follows:

   • **Path:** Choose from Unlocked or Locked. Choose Unlocked, and when you move the object, the path will move as well. Choose Locked, and when you move the object, the path will not move. Either option still enables you to edit or reposition the path.

   • **Smooth Start/Smooth End:** Select these check boxes, shown in Figure 14-11, to smooth out the movement of the animation as it enters or leaves the slide.

   • **Auto-Reverse:** The object will reverse the motion after completing the first motion.

   • **Sound:** Select a sound effect to attach to your animation. If you select Other Sound, navigate to your desired sound on your hard drive.

Figure 14-11: Add enhancements to your animation effects
Photo Credit: PhotoSpin

Figure 14-12: Specify your animation timing options
Photo Credit: PhotoSpin

- **After Animation:** Choose whether to dim or hide your text or object after the animation or after your next mouse click. You can also have your text or object change colors after the animation.

- **Animate Text:** Choose whether to have your text animate all at once or by each word or letter. If you choose by word or letter, specify the percentage of delay between words or letters.

7. In the dialog box for your specific animation effect, on the Timing tab, select the specific enhancements you want. For a motion path, your choices are as follows:

   - **Start:** Specify how you want the animation to begin, as shown in Figure 14-12. Choose from on mouse click, along with the previous animation, or after the previous animation plays through.

   - **Delay:** Specify whether you want a delay between the end of one animation and the beginning of the next.

   - **Speed:** Choose from a variety of speeds for your animation.

   - **Repeat:** Choose how many times you want the animation to loop (repeat).

   - **Rewind When Done Playing:** If you select this check box, the animation automatically rewinds when it's done playing and returns to its original state/position on the slide.

   - **Triggers:** Specify whether the animation plays when the mouse is just clicked or when the mouse is clicked on a specific object or piece of text.

8. Click OK.

9. Click Play, at the bottom of the pane, to preview the effect on your displayed slide. (See Figures 14-13 and 14-14.)

10. Click Slide Show, at the bottom of the pane, to play the presentation from your displayed slide forward.

Figure 14-13: The art moves in smoothly to a breeze sound effect . . .
Photo Credit: PhotoSpin

Figure 14-14: . . . and changes to a black silhouette
Photo Credit: PhotoSpin

Part IV
Presenting Effectively

Preparing the Presentation

*A*fter you've done all the hard work of compiling and formatting the content of your presentation, it's time to get it ready to share with the world. Begin by specifying the display options for your show. Determine how your show will be presented. Will a speaker control it, or will it be self-running on a kiosk? Choose whether your show will loop continuously and whether it will include narration and animation. Establish your timings and optimize your display performance.

When your show is ready to go, print your outline and all your notes and handouts. And last but not least, be sure to make a backup of your hard-earned presentation by packaging it to a CD. You want to be prepared if your original presentation stored on the computer's hard drive goes awry.

Chapter

15

Get ready to . . .

Set Up Your Show

1. Open a presentation in PowerPoint.

2. Click the Slide Show tab in the Ribbon.

3. Click Set Up Slide Show (see Figure 15-1).

4. In the Set Up Show dialog box, shown in Figure 15-2, specify the following settings:

   • **Show Type:** The Presented By A Speaker option displays a full-screen slide show that is controlled by a speaker. The Browsed By An Individual option displays in a window and is controlled by a user. Select the Show Scrollbar check box if you want the scroll bar to be visible for the user. The Browsed At A Kiosk option displays a full screen show that runs automatically.

   • **Show Options:** Select the Loop Continuously Until 'Esc' check box to enable the show to repeat continuously until you press Esc. Choose whether to run the show with narration and animation.

   • **Pen Color:** Select your desired pen color from the drop-down list.

   • **Show Slides:** By default, PowerPoint displays all your slides in the show. You can also specify a range of slides, if desired, by clicking the up and down arrows.

   • **Advance Slides:** See the sections "Set Timings for Slides Manually" and "Set Timings for Slides While Rehearsing" coming up in this chapter.

Figure 15-1: Click Set Up Slide Show

Figure 15-2: Specify your slide show options

 Remember to always double-check all your presentation hardware before giving your presentation. If possible, be sure to rehearse your presentation with the actual hardware you'll be using.

- **Multiple Monitors:** You can run your presentation on more than one monitor. From the drop-down menu, select the monitor to display PowerPoint and click Presenter View to view the slide show on the selected monitor.

- **Performance:** See the upcoming section, "Optimize Slide Show Performance," for details.

5. Click OK.

Remember to always double-check all your presentation hardware before giving your presentation. If possible, be sure to rehearse your presentation with the actual hardware you'll be using.

Set Timings for Slides Manually

1. Open a presentation in PowerPoint.

2. Click the Home tab.

3. Click the Slides pane and press Ctrl+A to select all slides.

4. Click the Animations tab.

5. Click the More button to open a drop-down menu (see Figure 15-3).

6. In the Slide Transition pop-up menu, select the transition effect you want to apply to all slides.

Note that you can select individual slides or groups of slides in a presentation and apply a transition effect. You can then select other slides and apply different transition effects.

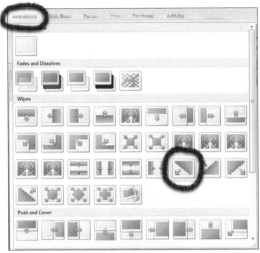

Figure 15-3: Open the Slide Transitions dialog box

Set Timings for Slides While Rehearsing

1. Open the presentation that you want to rehearse.

2. Click Slide Show in the Ribbon.

3. Click Rehearse Timings. Your slide show appears in what PowerPoint refers to as *rehearsal mode,* displayed in Full Screen mode with a clock showing elapsed time.

4. Practice your narration while the clock is moving and press the Page Down or right/down arrow key to move to the next slide. Continue scrolling through each slide as you rehearse the narration.

5. Press the Esc key when finished or press the Page Down or an arrow key to end the full screen view. A dialog box opens and asks you whether you want to accept the timings or start over. Click Yes, and your slides are displayed in a Slide Sorter view with the elapsed time between slides displayed in the Slide Sorter dialog box (see Figure 15-4).

Establish Print Options

1. Open a presentation in PowerPoint.

2. Click the Microsoft Office button and choose Print.

3. In the Print submenu, choose Print to open the Print dialog box.

4. Click Properties to open your printer driver Properties dialog box. Make choices for paper size, page orientation, and print attributes in the Printer Properties dialog box and click OK (see Figure 15-5) to return to the Print dialog box.

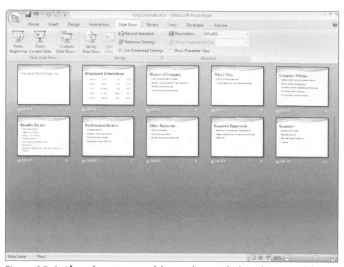

Figure 15-4: After rehearsing, your slides are shown with elapsed time per slide in the Slider Sorter view

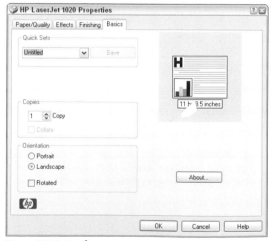

Figure 15-5: Specify your page orientation in the Printer Properties dialog box

Note that each printer has a unique set of options described in the Print Properties dialog box. Click the tabs and review all panes to become familiar with settings unique to your own desktop printer.

5. Select the page range in the Print dialog box (see Figure 15-6).

6. From the Print What drop-down list, choose an option to print. To print slides, select Slides.

7. Select a color mode. For proof prints select Grayscale from the Color/Grayscale drop-down list to conserve ink on color printers.

8. Click OK to print your slides.

Use Print Preview

1. Click the Microsoft Office button and choose Print.

2. From the Print submenu (see Figure 15-7), choose Print Preview to open the Print Preview window (see Figure 15-8).

3. Click Options to open the Options drop-down menu and choose options for:

   • **Header And Footer:** Select this option to open the Header And Footer dialog box. Enter your desired header and footer text in the Header And Footer dialog box. You can also choose to include the date and time in the header or footer. Check Slide number or Page number to have the number of the slide or page appear in the footer of the slide, notes page, or handout. Note that headers and footers on notes pages and handouts are separate from the headers and footers on slides.

Figure 15-6: Specify print attributes in the Print dialog box

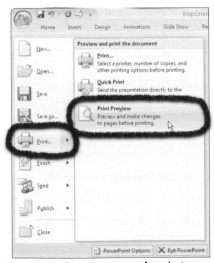

Figure 15-7: Choose Print Preview from the Print submenu

- **Color/Grayscale:** From the submenu, choose whether to print in Color (be sure you've chosen a color printer), Grayscale, or Pure Black And White. Choosing Pure Black And White results in no gray values in the print out.

- **Scale To Fit Paper:** If you select this option, slides will be sized to fit on your chosen paper size.

- **Frame Slides:** This option adds a frame around each printed slide.

- **Print Hidden Slides:** If you select this option, slides that you have designated to be hidden remain hidden but do print.

- **Print Comment And Ink Markup:** Select this option to enable reviewer comments and ink markups to print. For more on comments and ink markups, see Chapter 16.

- **Printing Order:** When printing handouts with 4, 6, or 0 slides, choose whether to print in order horizontally or vertically, from the submenu commands.

4. Click Print.

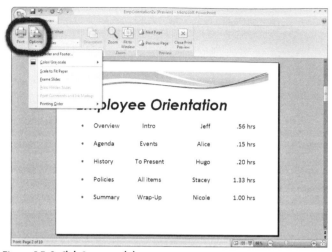

Figure 15-8: Click Options and choose a printing option

 Note that you can also set the preceding print options in the Print dialog box.

Print Audience Handouts

1. Open a presentation in PowerPoint.

2. Click the Microsoft Office button and choose Print➪ Print Preview.

3. On the Print Preview toolbar, select your desired Handout layout from the Print What drop-down menu. Choose 1, 2, 3, 4, 6, or 9 slides per page. Note that if you choose the 3-slide layout, as shown in Figure 15-9, blank lines are added next to each slide to allow for audience members to take notes during the presentation.

4. Specify additional print options as we describe in the earlier section, "Establish Print Options."

5. Click the Print button.

Print Speaker Notes

1. Open a presentation in PowerPoint.

2. Click the Microsoft Office button and choose Print➪ Print Preview

For a description on how to format speaker notes, see Chapter 6.

3. On the Print Preview toolbar, choose Notes Pages from the Print What drop-down menu, as shown in Figure 15-10. Each page prints with a single slide and the associated notes for that slide. (Speaker notes are helpful as references when delivering a presentation.)

4. Specify additional print options, as we describe in "Establish Print Options," earlier in this chapter.

5. Click the Print button.

Note that if you save your presentation as a Web page, your notes will be displayed by default. If you don't want them displayed, hide them before you save them. See Chapter 16 for details.

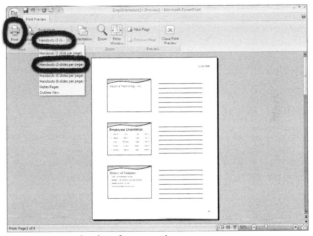

Figure 15-9: Print handouts for your audience

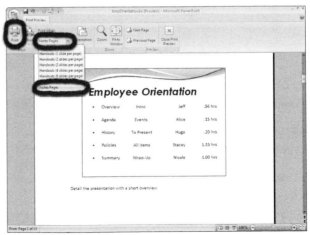

Figure 15-10: Print speaker notes

Print an Outline

1. Open a presentation in PowerPoint.

2. In the View tab, click Normal and click the Outline tab next to the Slides tab, as shown in Figure 15-11.

3. Open a context menu on a slide icon in Outline view and choose Expand⇨Expand all to expand all outline bullet points.

4. Click the Microsoft Office icon and choose Print⇨ Print Preview. On the Print Preview toolbar, choose Outline View from the Print What drop-down menu, as shown in Figure 15-12.

5. Specify additional print options, as we describe in the earlier section, "Establish Print Options."

6. Click the Print button.

 You may want to print your outline to use during a slide show to keep yourself on track as to what topics are coming up as you progress through your presentation. Using an outline allows you to have an overall global view of your presentation material. Note that when you have text on a slide specified as white text, PowerPoint automatically changes the text to black when you select Outline View in the Print Preview dialog box.

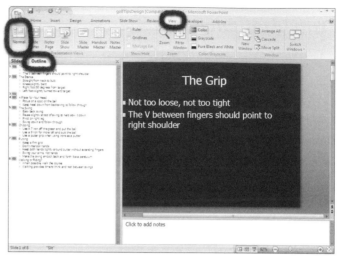

Figure 15-11: Expand your outline to display all text

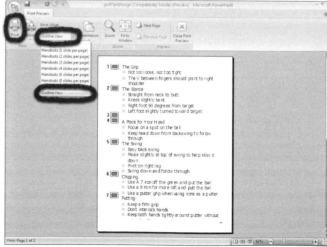

Figure 15-12: Print an outline

Send Handouts, Notes, or an Outline to Microsoft Word

1. Open a presentation in PowerPoint.

2. Click the Microsoft Office icon and choose PowerPoint Options.

3. Open the Commands Not In Ribbon menu and choose Send To Microsoft Word. Click the Add button to add the menu to the Quick Access Toolbar and click OK (see Figure 15-13).

4. Click the Send To Microsoft Office Word tool to open the Send To Microsoft Word dialog box, shown in 15-14. Select the desired page layout for your presentation:

   - **Notes Next To Slides:** Sets up a two-column layout with slides on the left and notes on the right.

   - **Blank Lines Next To Slides:** Sets up a two-column layout with blank lines adjacent to slides.

   - **Notes Below Slides:** Adds notes below each slide.

   - **Blank Lines Below Slides:** Adds blank lines below each slide.

   - **Outline Only:** Choose Outline Only to export the outline to a Word file.

    If you choose Handouts or Notes, specify whether you want to add the slides to Word as embedded files (Paste) or linked files (Paste link). Note that if you link the files, when you update them in PowerPoint, they'll also be updated in Word.

5. Click OK.

6. Your chosen presentation information appears as a new document in Word. Edit, format, and print the information as desired.

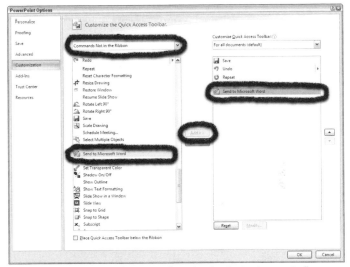

Figure 15-13: Add the Send To Microsoft Word tool to the Quick Access Toolbar

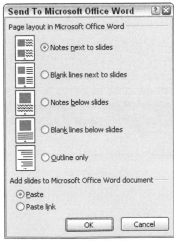

Figure 15-14: Specify what elements you want to send to Word

Optimize Slide Show Performance

1. Open a presentation in PowerPoint.

2. Click Slide Show in the Ribbon and click Set Up Slide Show (see Figure 15-15) to open the Set Up Show dialog box.

3. Under Performance, select the Use Hardware Graphics Acceleration check box, shown in Figure 15-16. If your graphics card supports this option, PowerPoint will implement it.

4. Under Performance, select 640 x 480 from the Slide Show Resolution drop-down list. Note that although this setting yields the fastest performance, it also yields the lowest fidelity, or quality. Click OK.

5. Click the View tab and click Slide Show to view your show with the edited settings. If you see any problems, go back to the default settings.

 Click the Tips button in the Set Up Show dialog box to get further information on how to improve slide show performance.

 Another thing you can do to improve the performance of the slide show is to work with your animations. Try reducing the size of your animated pictures. Also try to limit your use of animations that fade, rotate, or change size. Finally, limit your use of animated objects that include gradients or transparency.

Figure 15-15: Click Slide Show and click Set Up Slide Show

Figure 15-16: Improve your slide show performance if it appears sluggish

Create a Backup by Packaging for CD

1. Insert a blank CD into your drive.

2. Open the presentation that you want to package.

3. Make sure that your presentation is ready for packaging by reviewing all information. Remember to look at elements such as notes, comments, and ink annotations. If you don't want to include them, delete them now.

4. Click the Microsoft Office icon and choose Publish⟹ Package For CD (see Figure 15-17).

5. In the Package For CD dialog box, shown in Figure 15-18, name the CD by typing a name in the Name The CD text box.

6. If you want to add files that aren't automatically included in the packaging, click the Add Files button. In the Add Files dialog box that appears, navigate to and select your desired files. (Note that all linked files, along with the PowerPoint Viewer, are automatically included.) If you want to change the play order of the copied files, click the up or down arrows on the left of the dialog box. To remove a file, select it and click the Remove button. When you're done, click Add.

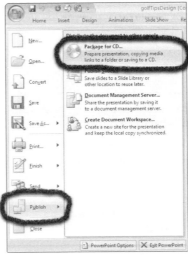

Figure 15-17: Choose Publish⟹Package For CD

Figure 15-18: Type a name for your CD package

7. Click the Options button to specify additional settings in the Options dialog box, shown in Figure 15-19:

   • Specify whether to make a self-running package. An XPS Viewer enables your presentation to play without using the PowerPoint application.

   • Specify how the presentations will play by selecting an option from the drop-down list. For example, you can enable the presentation a user wants to view.

   • Choose whether to embed TrueType fonts. Note that fonts that have built-in copyright protections won't be embedded.

   • To add a password requirement for opening or modifying the presentation, type your password in the corresponding field. Note that if any of the packaged files already have passwords (for example, PDF [Portable Document Format] or XPS [XML Paper Specification] files), PowerPoint asks you whether you want to keep those passwords or override them.

   • Check the box for Inspect Presentations For Inappropriate Or Private Information to ensure metadata in the file doesn't contain any information you want to prevent from distributing.

8. Click OK to exit the Option dialog box.

9. Click Copy To CD to write a CD.

 Note that the Package For CD command works only for Windows XP or later. For other operating systems, you can use the command only to copy your files to a folder. You can't copy them directly to a CD. To burn the files onto a CD, use your default CD burning application.

Figure 15-19: Specify your presentation CD options

 Always make a backup of your presentation onto other media, such as a USB jump drive or a CD. That way, you'll be prepared if the original file on your hard drive gets corrupted or you have some kind of computer glitch.

Sharing Your Presentation

Chapter 16

What good is a wonderful presentation if you don't share it with the world? PowerPoint offers you many ways to share. You can take the traditional and most personal route and present the show yourself (or choose a designated live body). If you're short on manpower or want to free up people for other tasks, you can present a self-running show. If you need feedback on a presentation, PowerPoint has a great system of sending a presentation out for review.

Need to collaborate? PowerPoint also provides a way, with the help of Microsoft Meeting Space, to hold online meetings. Finally, you can take the more technical route and share your presentation online via the Internet. This approach is a great way to disseminate information to a large audience or to people who are located in geographically diverse locations. This chapter gives you all you need to know to finalize your show and then share it with others.

Get ready to . . .

Use Office Diagnostics

1. Click the Microsoft Office icon to open the drop-down menu.

2. Choose PowerPoint Options to open the PowerPoint Options dialog box, shown in Figure 16-1.

3. Click Resources in the left pane.

4. Click Diagnose to the right of Office Diagnostics to open the Microsoft Office Diagnostics dialog box.

 All Microsoft Office programs have a self-healing feature that can detect and repair problems. When you run office diagnostics in any Office program, the Microsoft Office Diagnostics feature can often repair problems, such as failure to launch, frequent crashes, and features lost, that you may experience using the programs. When using features related to sharing files, you may have other programs in your Office suite that might have problems and are required to use a feature in PowerPoint. When you experience problems, your first effort at diagnosis and repair should be to use the steps outlined in this section.

5. Microsoft Office Diagnostics runs automatically when opening the Microsoft Office Diagnostics dialog box shown in Figure 16-2. Let the diagnosis finish before doing anything else on your computer.

6. Click Continue when the diagnosis is finished for repairs that can be made with Microsoft Office Diagnostics.

7. If you find links to Microsoft's Web site in the diagnosis repair reported in the Microsoft Office Diagnostics dialog box, click the links and view descriptions on how to repair problems.

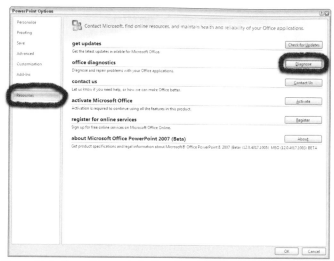

Figure 16-1: Choose Diagnose in the PowerPoint Options dialog box

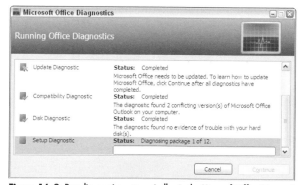

Figure 16-2: Run diagnostics automatically via the Microsoft Office Diagnostics dialog box

Create a Custom Show

1. Open a presentation in PowerPoint.

2. Click Slide Show in the Ribbon and click Custom Slide Show to open a drop-down menu. Choose Custom Shows from the menu to open the Custom Shows dialog box.

3. In the Custom Shows dialog box, shown in Figure 16-3, click New.

4. In the Define Custom Show dialog box, shown in Figure 16-4, select the slides you want to include in the custom show. Click Add.

5. If you need to change the order of the slides, click the slide you want to move to select it and then click the up or down arrow buttons on the right.

6. Give your custom show a name and click OK. The Custom Shows dialog box opens again and displays your new custom show, as shown in Figure 16-4.

7. Click Close to close the Custom Shows dialog box. Click Show to see a preview of the show. Note that you can also edit, remove, or copy your custom show by clicking the appropriate button on the right.

A *custom show* is simply a grouping of slides within your presentation that you can present separately from your main presentation or that you can hyperlink to. This can come in handy if you need to make presentations to several different groups within an organization. For example, everyone might need to view the main presentation, but you can create custom shows to present to individual groups that have slightly different needs.

Figure 16-3: Click Show to preview the new custom show

Figure 16-4: Define a custom show

To present a custom show, click Slide Show in the Ribbon and click Custom Slide Show to open the drop-down menu. From the menu choices, choose your custom slide show.

For details on hyperlinking to your custom show, see Chapter 13.

Set Permissions

1. Open a presentation in PowerPoint.

2. Click the Microsoft Office button to open the drop-down menu.

3. Choose Save As to open the Save As dialog box, shown in Figure 16-5.

4. Click Tools to open a pop-up menu and choose General Options to open the General Options dialog box.

5. In the General Options dialog box shown in Figure 16-6, choose from the following:

   • **Password To Open:** Type a password when you want to protect a presentation from being viewed by those without permissions.

   • **Password To Modify:** Type a password to prevent those without permissions from editing or changing your presentation.

   • **Privacy Options:** Check the box for Remove Automatically Created Personal Information From This File On Save to eliminate metadata containing privacy information.

   • **Macro Security:** Click this button to enable/disable macros.

You can add both a Password to open and a Password to modify when you want only those with permissions to view your file, but you don't want the viewers to modify the document.

6. Click OK, and a confirmation dialog box opens. Type your password(s) again to confirm and click OK to return to the General Options dialog box. Click OK in the General Options dialog box. Click Save in the Save As dialog box to save the file with encryption.

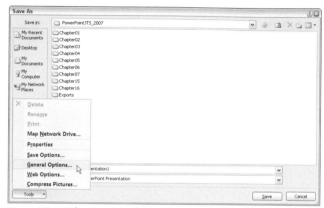

Figure 16-5: Select Save As and choose General Options in the Tools menu

Figure 16-6: Add a password to protect viewing and/or editing your presentation

Microsoft offers you another set of security options available through server-side Digital Rights Management. Open the Windows Office menu and choose Finish⇨Restrict Permission and choose from submenu commands for various encryption options. You need to subscribe to a service and use a Microsoft .NET account. A wizard walks you through steps to create a trial account and test the service before subscribing. For more information on this service, use the PowerPoint Help documents.

Use PowerPoint Viewer

1. If you downloaded and installed PowerPoint Viewer from the Web, choose Start⇨All Programs⇨Microsoft Office PowerPoint Viewer 2007.

2. Navigate to and select the presentation and click Open.

3. If you packaged PowerPoint viewer with the presentation by using the Package For CD command, navigate to that folder and double-click the PowerPoint viewer file (pptview.exe), as shown in Figure 16-7. In either case, your presentation automatically opens in a slide show view.

 PowerPoint Viewer is an application that enables you to run presentations without having PowerPoint installed. You must have PowerPoint Viewer installed on your computer before you or your recipients can use it. When you use the Package For CD feature, which we describe in Chapter 12, the Viewer is automatically installed. Otherwise, you can download it free of charge from Microsoft Office Online at http://office.microsoft.com.

Send a Presentation as an E-Mail Attachment

1. Open the presentation you want to save as an attachment.

2. Click the Microsoft Office icon to open the drop-down menu and choose Send.

3. Click Email in the submenu.

4. In the To and Cc fields, enter the e-mail addresses of your recipients, as shown in Figure 16-8. Type a message in the message area.

5. Click Send in the Ribbon.

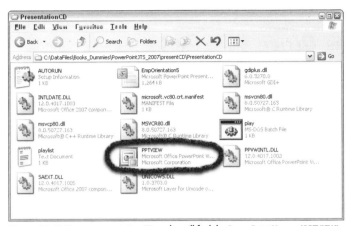

Figure 16-7: Open a presentation CD, and you'll find the PowerPoint Viewer (PPTVIEW)

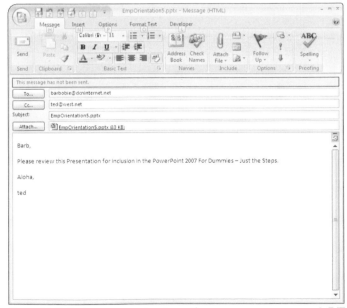

Figure 16-8: Send your presentation via e-mail

Save a Presentation as Office 97-2003

1. Open the presentation you want to share with users of Microsoft Office 97–2003.

2. Click the Microsoft Office icon to open the menu. Choose Save As to open the Save As submenu. (See Figure 16-9.)

3. Click PowerPoint 97–2003.

4. Type a name for your presentation and select a folder location on your hard drive. Click Save.

Review a Presentation

1. To review a presentation, double-click to open an e-mail attachment if a presentation is sent to you via e-mail.

2. Make any necessary changes in PowerPoint.

3. To add a comment, click the Review tab in the Ribbon and click New Comment. Type the comment in the sticky note added to your slide, as shown in Figure 16-10. Click outside the comment note, and the note collapses.

4. Additional tools available for commenting include

   • **Edit Comment**

   • **Delete**

   • **Previous**

   • **Next**

5. When you're done, e-mail the presentation back to the presentation author.

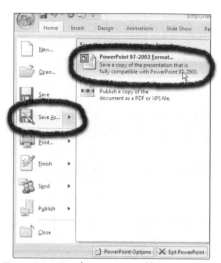

Figure 16-9: Attach a presentation like any other e-mail attachment

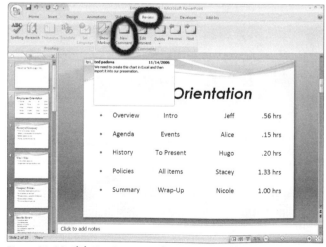

Figure 16-10: Click New Comment and start typing to add a comment

Save a Presentation as XML Paper Specification

1. Open a presentation in PowerPoint.

2. Click the Microsoft Office icon and click Save As.

3. Click PDF or XPS in the Save As submenu, as shown in Figure 16-11.

4. In the Publish As PDF Or XPS dialog box shown in Figure 16-12, make the following selections.

   - **File Name:** Type a filename for your XPS document.

   - **Save As Type:** By default, XPS Document appears as the file type. Leave the menu choice at the default.

   - **Open File After Publishing:** If you have an XPS viewer installed on your computer, the file opens in the XPS viewer after saving when this check box is checked.

   - **Standard (Publishing Online And Printing):** Check this box to preserve graphic image resolutions and keep the file optimized for printing.

   - **Minimum Size (Publishing Online):** For Web hosting and screen viewing, click this radio button to reduce file sizes.

   - **Options:** Click the Options button, and a number of choices are available similar to options you have when printing a PowerPoint file. You can choose the slides to export, choose note pages for exporting speaker notes, handouts for exporting audience handouts, or an outline view to export the outline text. Choose nonprinting metadata information and preserve permissions.

   - **Publish:** Click the Publish button to save the file in XPS format.

Figure 16-11: Click PDF or XPS to save a file in XPS format

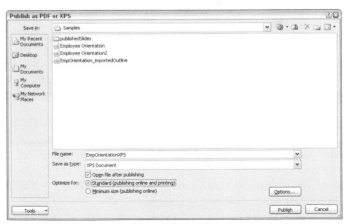

Figure 16-12: Choose Options for exporting to XPS

View an XML Paper Specification File

1. To open an XPS file, do one of the following:

   - **Open an XPS Viewer:** The Microsoft XML Paper Specification Viewer is installed with your Office applications. Open the XPS viewer and choose File➪Open to display the Open dialog box. Select an XPS file and click Open to open the file in the viewer, as shown in Figure 16-13.

   - **Open an XPS file in Microsoft Internet Explorer 7:** You can store XPS files locally on your hard drive or on the Web. When viewing Web-hosted XPS files, use Internet Explorer 7 to navigate to the URL where an XPS file is stored, and the file opens in Explorer 7.

2. Use the navigation buttons at the top of the toolbar to scroll pages or press the Up/Down Arrow keys on your keyboard. Alternately, you can type a number in the status bar and press Enter to jump to a page.

3. Click the Print tool or choose File➪Print to print the file.

4. Click in the Find box in the top right corner and type words to search in your file. Pres the Enter key after typing, and the viewer searches the document to find the next occurrence of a searched word.

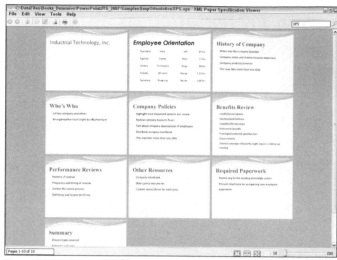

Figure 16-13: Open an XPS file in an XPS viewer

Transfer a Presentation to an FTP Site

1. Make sure that your computer is connected to the Internet and you have the proper FTP address and login and password information handy.

2. Open your presentation in PowerPoint.

3. Click the Microsoft Office button and choose Save As.

4. In the Save As dialog box, shown in Figure 16-14, type a URL address where you want to FTP your file

5. When the FTP site is accessed, navigate to the folder on the FTP server where you will be storing your presentation. Click Save.

  If your file is very large, saving it to an FTP site is a good way to transfer your file.

Figure 16-14: Save a presentation to a Web URL

Convert a Presentation to PDF

1. Open your presentation in PowerPoint.

2. Click the Microsoft Office icon and choose Save As from the drop-down menu.

3. Click PDF or XPS from the submenu to open the Publish As PDF Or XPS dialog box shown in Figure 16-15.

 Options you have after clicking the Options button are the same as you have when publishing an XPS file. See the section "Save a Presentation as an XML Paper Specification," earlier in this chapter.

4. Check the box for Open File After Publishing and click Publish.

 With Office 2007, you don't need Adobe Acrobat (Standard or Professional) or a PDF conversion tool to publish to PDF. PDF exports are built directly into all Office 2007 applications. You can export PowerPoint presentations to PDF complete with links, buttons, media, animations, and transitions. You can use any Acrobat Viewer as a slide presentation program that displays effects in Acrobat Viewer's full screen mode.

5. View the PDF file in an Acrobat Viewer, as shown in Figure 16-16.

 You must have Acrobat Viewer in order to view PDF files. You can download the free Adobe Reader software from Adobe Systems at `www.adobe.com/products/acrobat/ readermain.html`. If you don't have an Acrobat commercial product such as Acrobat Standard, Acrobat Professional, or Acrobat 3D, you can download a trial version good for 30 days by visiting `www.adobe.com/products/ acrobat`.

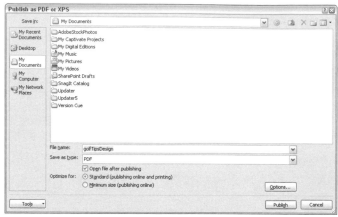

Figure 16-15: The Publish As PDF Or XPS dialog box

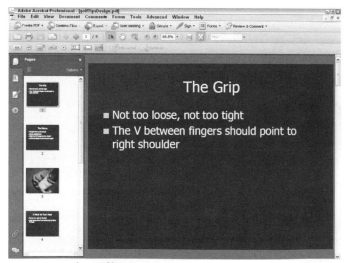

Figure 16-16: The PDF file in Acrobat Viewer

Add Metadata to PowerPoint Files

1. Open a presentation in PowerPoint.

2. Click the Microsoft Office icon and choose Finish from the drop-down menu.

3. Click Properties from the submenu to open the Properties Ribbon, shown in Figure 16-17.

 Document property information is stored as document metadata contained in your file and viewable in various dialog boxes and other areas, such as the Properties Ribbon. You can store document metadata in files that is useful with applications that can search metadata to help you quickly locate files on your hard drive or a server.

4. Add descriptions to the text boxes.

5. Click the Microsoft Office button and choose Save As. Save the file, and the document metadata records with the file save.

Create a Self-Running Kiosk

1. Open the presentation in PowerPoint.

2. Click the Slide Show tab in the Ribbon.

3. Click Set Up Slide Show in the Slide Show Ribbon to open the Set Up Show dialog box.

4. In the Set Up Show dialog box, shown in Figure 16-18, select the Browsed At A Kiosk (Full Screen) option. Be sure to add automatic timings so that the slides advance automatically. If you want users to control the show, add action buttons so that they can click to advance the slides. (For more on action buttons, see Chapter 11.)

Figure 16-17: Add document properties to your presentation

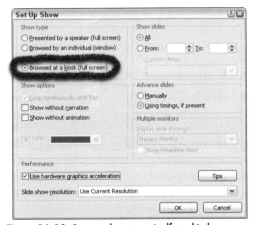

Figure 16-18: Create a show to run itself at a kiosk

Hold an Online Meeting

1. In PowerPoint, open the presentation you want to use in the meeting.

2. Click the Microsoft Office icon and choose PowerPoint Options. In the PowerPoint Options dialog box, open the Choose Custom Commands drop-down menu and scroll down to the Commands Not In Ribbon item. Click the Meet Now tool and click Add to add the tool to the Quick Access toolbar.

3. Click OK in the PowerPoint Options dialog box and click the Meet Now tool. Note that to participate in an online meeting, participants must have Microsoft Windows NetMeeting running on their computers. They must also be logged in to a directory server. If you've used NetMeeting before, proceed to Step 5.

4. If this is the first time you've used NetMeeting, you see the NetMeeting dialog box. Enter your information. Click OK.

5. In the Find Someone dialog box, shown in Figure 16-19, select the directory server that your desired participants are logged in to from the Select a Directory drop-down list. Select a participant's name from the list. Click Call. Repeat this process for all your desired participants.

6. Click Close to close the Find Someone dialog box. Any participants who have accepted the meeting request will appear in the Participants list on the Online Meeting toolbar that appears when you close the dialog box.

Figure 16-19: Select your meeting participants in the Find Someone dialog box

For users of Adobe Reader or Adobe Acrobat, a similar type of meeting button appears in all Acrobat 8 viewers. If you routinely work between Office applications and Acrobat, click the Start Meeting button to create a free trial account with Acrobat Connect. Acrobat Connect enables you to host your own personal meeting room where up to 15 users can view any document on your computer via their Web browser.

Access Files Quickly

1. Launch Microsoft Internet Explorer 7.

 You can open any file you see in the desktop view directly in the original authoring program by double-clicking the file icon. If you download files from the Web to a folder or you work in several applications and don't have a handy view of folders on the desktop, you can let Explorer be your navigation guide and open files in Explorer that are immediately routed to the original authoring program or displayed as inline views in the Explorer window.

2. Choose File➪Open to display the Explorer Open dialog box, shown in Figure 16-20.

3. Click Browse to open the Windows Internet Explorer dialog box. Click All Files from the Files Of Type drop-down menu and navigate to a location and select a file to open. Your choices include

   - **PowerPoint:** PowerPoint files selected in Explorer open the files directly in PowerPoint.

   - **Word:** Word files selected in Explorer open the files directly in Word.

   - **Excel:** Excel files selected in Explorer open the files directly in Excel.

   - **XPS:** XPS files open in Explorer as inline views, as shown in Figure 16-21.

   - **PDF:** PDF Files open in Explorer as inline views in the Explorer window. Your Acrobat Viewer has preference options to toggle the views between inline views and opening files in an Acrobat Viewer.

4. Click Open, and the selected file opens in the application according to the file type.

Figure 16-20: Click Browse to locate a file to open

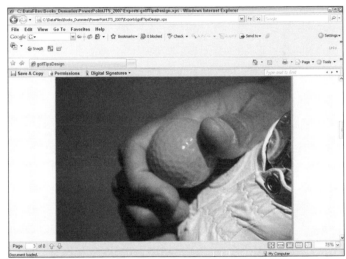

Figure 16-21: XPS files open in Explorer as inline views in the Web browser window

Index

• K •

• L •

• M •

Notes